C29 0000 0603 497

D1765711

The Language Experts

GERMAN2.0

The Interactive Language Course for the 21st Century

APA Publications (UK) Limited

New York   London   Singapore

GERMAN2.0

NO part of this book may be reproduced, stored in a retrieval system or transmitted in any form or means electronic, mechanical, photocopying, recording or otherwise, without prior written permission from APA Publications.

Contacting the Editors

Every effort has been made to provide accurate information in this publication, but changes are inevitable. The publisher cannot be responsible for any resulting loss, inconvenience or injury. We would appreciate it if readers would call our attention to any errors or outdated information by contacting Berlitz Publishing, e-mail: comments@berlitzpublishing.com

All Rights Reserved
©2011 APA Publications (UK) Limited

Berlitz Trademark Reg. U.S. Patent Office and other countries. Marca Registrada. Used under license from Berlitz Investment Corporation.

Mac is a trademark of Apple Inc., registered in the U.S. and other countries.

First Printing: August 2011
Printed in China

Publishing Director: Sheryl Olinsky Borg
Senior Editor/Project Manager: Lorraine Sova
Editorial: Julia Krumme, Silke Grauenhorst, Andrea Pearman, Dr. Steve Williams, Sabine Amoss, Rosi McNab, Saskia Gorospe Rombouts, Sylvia Goulding, Peter Kellersman, Elvira Oritz, Joachim Siebert
Cover and Interior Design: Leigha
Interior Composition: Wee Design
Cover Photo: Alexander Raths.Sh
Production Manager: Elizabeth Ga

FLINTSHIRE SIR Y FFLINT	
C29 0000 0603 497	
ASKEWS & HOLT	21-Jul-2011
438.2421	£19.99
CQ	

Contents

How to Use GERMAN2.0

GERMAN2.0 is an innovative, beginner-level course that features a multimedia approach to help you function in a wide variety of everyday situations with German speakers. You'll practice listening, speaking, reading and writing in German online and by following the book.

 Visit the 2.0 companion website, **www.berlitzhotspot.com**, for all online and downloadable content.

GERMAN2.0 is divided into 18 lessons. Each lesson focuses on an important theme, such as greetings and introductions, ordering food and shopping. The lessons include these features:

DIALOGUE

Real-life dialogues between native speakers

VOCABULARY

The lesson's key words and phrases

ACTIVITY

A fun way to practice your listening, speaking, reading and writing skills— in the book and online

DID YOU KNOW?

Cultural aspects of the major German-speaking countries

GRAMMAR

Quick and easy grammar explanations— in plain English

LEARNING TIP

Advice on how to remember your new language

PRONUNCIATION

A focus on the sounds of German

LEARN MORE

Practical ways to extend your language skills

 Check It!

A useful list of what you've accomplished in the lesson

BERLITZ HOTSPOT

Go to www.berlitzhotspot.com for...

Social Networking
Prompts to start conversations
with your Hotspot friends

Podcast
Downloadable info on
German culture and language

Internet Activity
Explore real German websites

Video
Animated scenes of German gestures and situations

Audio
For sections that are available with audio

You'll also find two tests in the book, after lessons 9 and 18. The tests are
an opportunity to confirm you've met the goals of the course. And, for your
reference, an answer key has been included.

GERMAN2.0 CD-ROM

In addition to online content, 2.0 includes a CD-ROM, at the back
of this book, with fun language-learning games, activities and
audio. Practice and reinforce the language you're learning!

Match It!
Play a German-language
memory game.

Quiz2.0
Test your knowledge
of German language,
grammar and culture.

Watch It!
Answer questions about
the German2.0 videos.

Listen Up!
Advance your listening
comprehension skills.

Speak Up!
Practice your German
pronunciation.

Pronunciation

This section is designed to make you familiar with the sounds of German, using our simplified phonetic transcription. You'll find the pronunciation of the German letters explained below, together with their "imitated" equivalents.

The German alphabet is the same as English, with the addition of the letter **ß**. Some vowels appear with an **Umlaut**: **ä**, **ü** and **ö**. Of note, German recently underwent a spelling reform. The letter **ß** is now shown as **ss** after a short vowel, but is unchanged after a long vowel or diphthong. In print and dated material, you may still see the **ß** after short vowels; e.g., formerly **Kuß**, now **Kuss**.

Stress has been indicated in the phonetic transcription: the underlined letters should be pronounced with more stress than others, e.g., **Adresse**, **ah-drehs-uh**.

CONSONANTS

Letter	Approximate Pronunciation	Symbol	Example	Pronunciation
b	1. at the end of a word or between a vowel and a consonant, like p in up	p	ab	ahp
b	2. elsewhere, as in English	b	bis	bihs
c	1. before e, i, ä and ö, like ts in hits	ts	Celsius	tsehl-zee-oos
c	2. elsewhere, like c in cat	k	Café	kah-feh
ch	1. like k in kit	k	Wachs	vahks
ch	2. after vowels, like ch in Scottish loch	kh	doch	dohkh
d	1. at the end of the word or before a consonant, like t in eat	t	Rad	raht
d	2. elsewhere, like d in do	d	danke	dahn-kuh
g	1. at the end of a word, sounds like k	k	fertig	fehr-teek
g	2. like g in go	g	gehen	geh-uhn
j	like y in yes	y	ja	yah
qu	like k + v	kv	Quark	kvahrk
r	pronounced in the back of the mouth	r	warum	vah-room

Letter	Approximate Pronunciation	Symbol	Example	Pronunciation
s	1. before or between vowels, like z in zoo	z	sie	zee
s	2. before p and t, like sh in shut	sh	Sport	shpohrt
s	3. elsewhere, like s in sit	s	es ist	ehs ihst
ß	like s in sit	s	groß	grohs
sch	like sh in shut	sh	schnell	shnehl
tsch	like ch in chip	ch	deutsch	doych
tz	like ts in hits	ts	Platz	plahts
v	1. like f in for	f	vier	feer
v	2. in foreign words, like v in voice	v	Vase	vah-suh
w	like v in voice	v	wie	vee
z	like ts in hits	ts	zeigen	tsie-gehn

Letters f, h, k, l, m, n, p, t and x are pronounced as in English.

VOWELS

Letter	Approximate Pronunciation	Symbol	Example	Pronunciation
a	like a in father	ah	Tag	tahk
ä	1. like e in let	eh	Lärm	lehrm
ä	2. like a in late	ay	spät	shpayt
e	1. like e in let	eh	schnell	shnehl
e	2. at the end of a word, if the syllable is not stressed, like u in us	uh	bitte	biht-tuh
i	1. like i in hit, before a doubled consonant	ih	billig	bih-leek
i	2. otherwise, like ee in meet	ee	ihm	eem
o	like o in home	oh	voll	fohl
ö	like er in fern	er	schön	shern
u	like oo in boot	oo	Nuss	noos
ü	like ew in new	ew	über	ew-behr
y	like ew in new	ew	typisch	tew-peesh

Combined Vowels

Letter	Approximate Pronunciation	Symbol	Example	Pronunciation
ai, ay, ei, ey	like ie in tie	ie	nein	nien
ao, au	like ow in now	ow	auf	owf
äu, eu, oy	like oy in boy	oy	neu	noy

Lesson 1   Hello.

Guten Tag.

Lesson 1 is about getting to know people. When you have completed this lesson, you'll know how to:

- exchange greetings
- introduce yourself
- ask how someone is doing

DIALOGUE

 Listen to several people greeting each other.

1

Herr Schmidt:	**Tag, Frau Schultz.** Hello Mrs. Schultz.
Frau Schultz:	**Ach, guten Tag, Herr Schmidt.** Oh, hello Mr. Schmidt.

2

Frau Andresen:	**Guten Tag, Herr Haase.** Hello, Mr. Haase.
Herr Haase:	**Guten Morgen, Frau Andresen.** Good morning, Mrs. Andresen.

3

Frau:	**Auf Wiedersehen, Herr Hartmann.** Goodbye, Mr. Hartmann.
Herr Hartmann:	**Wiedersehen.** Bye.

4

Frau Schultz:	**Guten Abend, Herr Hartmann.** Good evening, Mr. Hartmann.
Herr Hartmann:	**Guten Abend, Frau Schultz.** Good evening, Mrs. Schultz.

5

Joachim:	**Tschüs!** Bye!
Frau:	**Tschüs, Joachim.** Bye, Joachim.

6

Astrid:	**Gute Nacht, Gisela.** Good night, Gisela.
Gisela:	**Gute Nacht, Astrid.** Good night, Astrid.

1. DIALOGUE ACTIVITY

A. **Which dialogues include a hello and which ones include a goodbye?**

B. **Can you tell what time of day it is in each conversation?**

Use the following words and expressions to guide you through the lesson.

VOCABULARY

Abend	evening	**ist**	is
ach	oh	**mein**	my
auch	also	**mich**	me
Auf Wiederhören.	Goodbye (on the phone).	**Morgen**	morning
		Nacht	night
Auf Wiedersehen.	Goodbye.	**Name**	name
danke	thank you	**sehr gut**	very well
es	it	**Sie**	you (for.)
Familienname	surname; last name	**Tag**	day
		Tschüs!	Bye! (inf.)
Frau	Mrs./Ms.	**und**	and
Freut mich!	Pleased to meet you! (lit.: Pleases me!)	**Und Ihnen?**	And you?
		Versuchen Sie es!	You try it!
gut	good, well	**Vorname**	first name
Gute Nacht!	Good night!	**wie**	how
Guten Abend!	Good evening!	**Wie bitte?**	I'm sorry?/ Pardon? (lit.: How please?)
Guten Morgen!	Good morning!		
Guten Tag!	Hello, good morning/afternoon!	**Wie geht es Ihnen?**	How are you? (for.)
Hallo!	Hi!	**Wie geht's?**	How are you? (inf.)
Herr	Mr.		
ich	I	**Wie ist Ihr Familienname/ Vorname?**	What's your last name/first name?
ich heiße	I'm (called)/my name is		
Ich kann nicht klagen.	I can't complain.	**Wie kann ich Ihnen helfen?**	How can I help you?
Ihnen	(to) you		

Guten Tag!

Wie geht es Ihnen?

Abbreviations

f. feminine
for. formal
inf. informal
lit. literally
m. masculine
pl. plural
s. singular

2. LISTENING ACTIVITY

Listen to these greetings and practice saying them to yourself. Then fill in the chart as to when it is appropriate to use each.

Guten Tag!

Guten Morgen!

Guten Abend!

Auf Wiedersehen!

Tschüs!

Gute Nacht!

Any Time of Day	Morning	Evening	Night

DID YOU KNOW?

Most greetings can be shortened:

Guten Tag.	→	Tag.
Guten Morgen.	→	Morgen.
Guten Abend.	→	Abend.
Auf Wiedersehen.	→	Wiedersehen.

3. SPEAKING ACTIVITY

Look at the images below. For each, make up a short greeting/farewell using the information given.

1   **Frau Unsinn**   **Christian**

2   **Herr Springer**   **Florian**

3   **Werner**   **Bernd**

4   **Sandra**   **Helen**

DID YOU KNOW?

To introduce yourself in German you can use a greeting, like *Guten Tag*, and then say *Ich heiße* … (I am called) followed by your name. To respond to a greeting, you can say: *Freut mich*, which means pleased to meet you. If you are the second person in the conversation to introduce yourself, you can add *auch* (also), as in *Freut mich auch* (pleased to meet you, too).

4. SPEAKING ACTIVITY

Now practice introducing yourself and responding to introductions like in the following example.

Sie: **Guten Tag. Ich heiße** _____.

insert your name

Thomas: **Freut mich ... Ich heiße Thomas.**

Sie: **Freut mich auch.**

DID YOU KNOW?

In German-speaking countries it's normal to shake hands when meeting someone.

5. LISTENING ACTIVITY

Listen to people greeting each other in German. Match the person on the left with the person he or she is greeting, on the right.

a. Guten Tag. Ich heiße Fritz Knoll.

1. Ich heiße Horst Henneberg.

b Guten Abend. Gisela Kalisch.

2. Irene Pfaff. Freut mich.

c. Guten Tag. Ich heiße Birgit Walther.

3. Bernd Krüger. Freut mich.

1

Frau Walther: **Guten Tag. Ich heiße Birgit Walther.** Hello, I am Birgit Walther.
Herr Henneberg: **Ich heiße Horst Henneberg.** I am Horst Henneberg.

2

Herr Knoll: **Guten Tag. Ich heiße Fritz Knoll.** Hello, my name is Fritz Knoll.
Herr Krüger: **Bernd Krüger. Freut mich.** I'm Bernd Krüger. Pleased to meet you.

3

Frau Kalisch: **Guten Abend. Gisela Kalisch.** Good evening. I'm Gisela Kalisch.
Frau Pfaff: **Irene Pfaff. Freut mich.** I'm Irene Pfaff. Pleased to meet you.

6. WRITING ACTIVITY

You are checking into a hotel. Fill the gaps with appropriate responses.

Empfangschefin: **Guten Tag. Wie kann ich Ihnen helfen?**

Sie: [_____].

Greeting

Ich [_____].

Give your name.

Empfangschefin: **Wie bitte? Wie ist Ihr Familienname?**

Sie: **Mein** [_____] **ist**

[_____].

Empfangschefin: **Und Ihr Vorname?**

Sie: **Mein** [_____] **ist**

[_____].

Empfangschefin: **Danke.**

7. WRITING ACTIVITY

Fill in the gaps in this conversation between Herr Schmidt and his colleague, Herr Hartmann.

Herr Schmidt: **Guten Tag, Herr Hartmann! Wie** [_____]

[_____] [_____] **?**

Herr Hartmann: **Sehr** [_____] **,** [_____] **.**

Und [_____] **?**

Herr Schmidt: **Ach, ich kann nicht klagen.**

GRAMMAR

The Letter ß

The letter *ß* indicates a sharper "s" sound. Its pronunciation is similar to the ss in English. Usually the *ß* is preceded by a long vowel (e.g., *Straße, Fuß,* etc.). *Ss* is used when it is preceeded by a short vowel (*Wasser, Kasse*), in upper case words (*FUSS*), or when typewriters and keyboards are not equipped with the *ß* letter.

Verbs

When you look up verbs in a dictionary, you'll notice that most of them end in *-en*. (This verb form is called the infinitive.) For example: *heißen* is the verb "to be called."

However, "I am called" is *ich heiße*—without the *-n*! This is because the ending of a German verb changes according to whether the subject is "I," "we," "you," "he/she/it" or "they," which you will learn more about in future lessons.

DID YOU KNOW?

When you run into somebody you know it's polite to ask how they are: *Wie geht es Ihnen?* This literally means, "How goes it to you." You can answer: *Gut, danke. Und Ihnen?* Which means, "Fine, thanks. And you?" If you're feeling really cheerful you can answer: *Sehr gut, danke.* "Very well, thanks."

Check It!

Test what you've learned in this lesson and review anything you're not sure of.

CAN YOU . . . ?

☐ **greet someone in the morning, afternoon and evening**
Guten Morgen!
Guten Tag!
Guten Abend!

☐ **say goodbye to someone**
(Auf) Wiedersehen!
Tschüs!

☐ **say good night**
Gute Nacht!

☐ **introduce yourself**
Ich heiße …

☐ **ask how someone is**
Wie geht es Ihnen?
Wie geht's?

 BERLITZ HOTSPOT   Go to www.berlitzhotspot.com for…

 Social Networking
Go to the **Berlitz Hotspot** page. Meet new friends learning German just like you. Share what you've learned, ask questions, trade tips, find photos and more!

 Podcast 1
Nice to meet you.
Or not!
Download this podcast

 Internet Activity
Are you interested in learning more German names? Go to **Berlitz Hotspot** for a list of sites with German names. Browse and pick three or four names you like. Practice saying those names. Try saying *Ich heiße …* in front of each one.

 Video 1 – Meeting Someone for the First Time
Two Germans are meeting each other for the first time. What do they say? What do they do? Watch the video and find out how German speakers greet each other.

Wie ist Ihre Nummer?

LESSON OBJECTIVES

Lesson 2 is about the letters and numbers. When you have completed this lesson, you'll know how to:

- spell your name
- count to 10
- talk on the telephone

DIALOGUE

🔊 Listen as some people are asked what their names are, *Wie ist Ihr Name?*, and how their names are spelled, *Können Sie das bitte buchstabieren?*

1

 Wie ist Ihr Name, bitte? What's your name, please?

Mein Name ist Steuer. My name is Steuer.

 Können Sie das buchstabieren, bitte? Can you spell that, please?

S-T-E-U-E-R, Steuer.

2

 Wie heißen Sie? What's your name, please?

Ich heiße Thomas Gross. I'm Thomas Gross.

 Können Sie das buchstabieren, bitte? Can you spell that, please?

Ja. G-R-O-S-S, Gross.

3

 Wie ist Ihr Name? What's your name?

Mein Name ist Konstanze Schmäh. My name is Konstanze Schmäh.

 Können Sie das buchstabieren, bitte? Can you spell that, please?

S-C-H-M-A-Umlaut-H, Schmäh.

4

 Wie heißen Sie? What's your name?

Ich heiße Bernd Schmitt. I am Bernd Schmitt.

 Mit DT oder mit Doppel-T? With DT or with a double T?

Mit Doppel-T: S-C-H-M-I-T-T.

Use the following words and expressions to guide you through the lesson.

VOCABULARY

buchstabieren	to spell	**natürlich**	of course, naturally
erreichen	to reach	**nein**	no
Es tut mir leid.	I'm sorry.	**neu**	new
hier	here	**nicht**	not
im Moment	at the moment	**Nummer**	number
ja	yes	**spricht**	speaks, is speaking
kann (er/sie/es kann)	can (he/she/it can)		
		wiederholen	to repeat
können (Sie können)	can (you can, for.)	**zuhören**	to listen
		zurückrufen	to call back
Magazin	magazine		

1. DIALOGUE ACTIVITY

What are the names of the people in the dialogues?

\[\]

\[\]

\[\]

\[\]

DID YOU KNOW?

Have you noticed that German has an accent in the writing? Two dots above A, O, or U, which change the sound of those vowels. The name for this accent is the *Umlaut*, so when you hear the letter *A-Umlaut* (ä), the letter *O-Umlaut* (ö), or the letter *U-Umlaut* (ü), you'll know to write the two dots above the vowel. The special form for -ss is called *ß* (Eszett) or *scharfes*, sharp -S.

2. SPEAKING ACTIVITY

Listen to the German alphabet. Repeat the letters and try to pronounce them like the speaker.

German Alphabet

A B C D E F G

H I J K L M N

O P Q R S T U

V W X Y Z

3. LISTENING ACTIVITY

Circle the names below that you hear spelled.

Erika
Hannelore
Karl
Käthe
Kerstin

Klaus
Peter
Petra
Sabine
Sibylle

Susanne
Sylvia
Walter
Werner

Now look again at the names you have circled and try to spell them out loud.

4. SPEAKING ACTIVITY

Spell your own first name and last name out loud in German.

5. LISTENING ACTIVITY

Listen to the numbers 0-10. Repeat them aloud to yourself. Really make an effort to imitate the speaker.

0	null	3	drei	6	sechs	9	neun
1	eins	4	vier	7	sieben	10	zehn
2	zwei/zwo*	5	fünf	8	acht		

* *Zwo* is used when giving numbers on the phone, to avoid confusion with *drei*.

6. LISTENING ACTIVITY

Which of these business cards belong to the people taking part in the telephone conversation?

Herr Schulz:	Tempo Magazin. Guten Tag.
Frau Lenz:	Guten Tag. Sind Sie Herr Dittmann?
Herr Schulz:	Nein, ich bin Dieter Schulz. Herr Dittmann ist im Moment nicht hier. Wie ist Ihr Name, bitte?
Frau Lenz:	Petra Lenz.
Herr Schulz:	Können Sie das buchstabieren, bitte?
Frau Lenz:	Ja. L-E-N-Z, Lenz.
Herr Schulz:	Danke. Wie ist Ihre Nummer?
Frau Lenz:	030 319 1510.
Herr Schulz:	Danke, Frau Lenz. Auf Wiederhören.
Frau Lenz:	Auf Wiederhören.

7. SPEAKING ACTIVITY

It's your turn! Imagine that you are phoning Tempo Magazin. You want to speak to Herr Schulz. Make sure that you can spell your name and give your phone number in German before you play the recording.

Herr Dittmann:	Tempo Magazin. Guten Tag.
Sie:	Greet the speaker and ask if the speaker is Mr. Schulz.
Herr Dittmann:	Nein, hier ist Hans Dittmann. Herr Schulz ist nicht hier. Wie ist Ihr Name, bitte?
Sie:	Give your name.
Herr Dittmann:	Können Sie das buchstabieren, bitte?
Sie:	Spell your name.
Herr Dittmann:	Danke. Wie ist Ihre Nummer?
Sie:	Give your telephone number.
Herr Dittmann:	Danke. Auf Wiederhören.
Sie:	Say goodbye.

8. **LISTENING ACTIVITY**

Listen to the answering machine messages, and then look at Gisela Braun's phone pad. Correct any numbers that are wrong.

A-Z Versicherung
   3|4 88|8

Herzog, Marion
   3|3 2900

Pfaff, Gudrun
   8|5 7482

Schmidt, Rudi
   782 4|4|

Herr Schmidt: **Guten Tag, Frau Braun. Hier ist Andreas Schmidt von A-Z Versicherung. Meine Nummer ist drei - eins - vier - acht - neun - eins - neun. Danke.**

Frau Herzog: **Hallo Gisela. Wie geht's? Hier spricht Marion. Marion Herzog. Meine neue Nummer ist acht - neun - vier - sieben - zwei - acht - zwei. Tschüs.**

Rudi: **Hi. Ich bin's. Rudi. Ich bin unter sieben - acht - zwei - null - vier - null - sieben zu erreichen. Ciao.**

Frau Pfaff: **Guten Tag, Frau Braun. Hier ist Gudrun Pfaff. Meine Nummer ist acht - eins - fünf - sieben - vier - acht - zwei. Wiederhören.**

Capital letters

Capitals are used more frequently in German than in English. They are used:

- at the beginning of a sentence (as in English)

- for proper nouns, e.g., people's names (as in English)

- for all other nouns, e.g., *Name* "name," *Tag* "day"

- for *Sie*, "you," *Ihnen*, "to you," and *Ihr*, "your"

The word for "I"—*ich*—doesn't have a capital (unless it comes at the beginning of a sentence).

9. WRITING ACTIVITY

Mark which words in these sentences should begin with a capital letter.

a. guten tag. mein name ist henneberg – horst henneberg.

b. guten abend, herr schmidt! wie geht es ihnen?

c. guten morgen. ich bin fritz knoll.

d. kommen sie herein.

Regular Verb Endings

To use a verb with a subject in a sentence, you have to change the form of that verb (conjugate). In many cases, you take the *-en* ending off the infinitive, leaving the stem of the verb, then add the appropriate ending for the subject. For example, the verb "to be called" in German is *heißen*. The stem of *heißen* is *heiß-*. If you want to say "I am called," you add the ending *-e* to the stem: *ich heiße*. Here is the full present tense of *heißen*:

Singular

ich heiße	I am called
du heißt	you (inf.) are called
Sie heißen	you (for.) are called
er/sie/es heißt	he/she/it is called

Plural

wir heißen	we are called
ihr heißt	you (inf.) are called
Sie heißen	you (for.) are called
sie heißen	they are called

These verb endings are the same for almost all verbs—so you only have to learn them once.

10. WRITING ACTIVITY

Try to practice the forms of some of the verbs you have learned in this lesson.

1 **buchstabieren** to spell

   a. ich

   b. Sie

   c. wir

2 **wiederholen** to repeat

   a. ihr

   b. sie (sing.)

   c. du

3 **zuhören** to listen

   a. du

   b. er

   c. ich

4 **zurückrufen** to call back

   a. sie (sing.)

   b. Sie

   c. wir

11. WRITING ACTIVITY

Can you conjugate *heißen* in all of its forms?

Singular

Plural

12. SPEAKING ACTIVITY

Leave a message for Frau Braun on her answering machine. Greet her. Tell her who you are. Leave your number, etc. Try to incorporate as many new structures and vocabulary words as you can.

Check It!

Test what you've learned in this lesson and review anything you're not sure of.

CAN YOU . . . ?

☐ **recite the alphabet**
A, B, C, D …

☐ **spell your name**

☐ **count from 0 to 10**
null, eins, zwei …

☐ **give your phone number**

☐ **ask whether you are speaking to a certain person**
Sind Sie Herr Schulz?

☐ **ask for someone to phone you back**
Kann er/sie mich zurückrufen?

☐ **conjugate regular verbs**

ich heiße	wir heißen
du heißt	ihr heißt
Sie heißen	Sie heißen
er/sie/es heißt	sie heißen

Go to www.berlitzhotspot.com for…

BERLITZ HOTSPOT

Social Networking
Introduce yourself at the **Berlitz Hotspot**. Use this model: *Tag, ich heiße* (your name).

Podcast 2
Hello!
Download this podcast.

Internet Activity
Would you like more practice learning to spell? Go to the lists of names at **Berlitz Hotspot**. Practice spelling them aloud.

Lesson 3 — Are You From...?

Kommen Sie aus ... ?

LESSON OBJECTIVES

Lesson 3 is about saying where you're from and introducing people. When you have completed this lesson, you'll know how to:

- say where you come from
- make introductions
- count to 20

DIALOGUE

  Listen to these people introduce themselves and say where they are from.

Herr Schwarz: **Guten Tag. Mein Name ist Harald Schwarz und ich komme aus Wien, Österreich.**
Hello, my name is Harald Schwarz and I'm from Vienna, Austria.

Frau Müller: **Servus. Ich bin Sara Müller. Ich komme aus München in Bayern.**
Hi. I am Sara Müller. I'm from Munich, in Bavaria.

Frau Hansen: **Hi. Ich bin Petra Hansen. Ich komme aus Kiel in Schleswig-Holstein.**
Hi. I'm Petra Hansen. I'm from Kiel, Schleswig-Holstein.

Herr Krüger: **Ich heiße Peter Krüger und ich komme aus Berlin. Hallo!**
My name is Peter Krüger and I'm from Berlin. Hello!

1. DIALOGUE ACTIVITY

A. **Which city is each person from?**

B. **Do you know these city names in English?**

Use the following words and expressions to guide you through the lesson.

VOCABULARY

auf	on	**minus**	minus
aus	from, out (of)	**München**	Munich
ausgezeichnet	excellent; very well	**Österreich**	Austria
Bayern	Bavaria (German state)	**plus**	plus
		Polen	Poland
Bern	Berne	**recht gut**	quite well
Darf ich ... vorstellen?	May I introduce...?	**Schleswig-Holstein**	Schleswig-Holstein (state in northern Germany)
das	this; that		
Das ist ...	This/That is...	**Servus!**	Hello! (southern German/ Austrian greeting and farewell)
dürfen (ich darf)	may		
Geschäftsreise	business trip		
Ich bin auf Geschäftsreise.	I'm on a business trip.	**Sind Sie von hier?**	Are you from here?
		und	and
Ich komme aus ...	I'm from...	**Urlaub**	vacation
im	in the	**von**	from, of
Köln	Cologne	**vorstellen**	to introduce
kommen	to come	**Wien**	Vienna
Land	German state, country	**woher**	where, from
Mein Name ist ...	My name is...	**Woher kommen Sie?**	Where are you from?

DID YOU KNOW?

If you find *die Vereinigten Staaten* to be a bit of a mouthful at the moment, you can always say *die USA*.

2. LISTENING ACTIVITY

 Listen to the dialogue again and match each person to their city on the map.

Harald Schwarz

Sara Müller

Peter Krüger

Petra Hansen

3. WRITING ACTIVITY

Did you notice in the dialogue how each person said where they were from? They used the phrase: *Ich komme aus ...* (I'm from..., lit. I come from...). *Kommen* (to come) is a regular verb. Try conjugating writing in the verb endings. Refer back to Lesson 2 if you don't remember all the verb endings.

ich komm		**wir komm**	
du komm		**ihr komm**	
Sie komm		**sie (pl.) komm**	
er/sie/es komm			

4. **LISTENING ACTIVITY**

Where are these people from? Write out the complete sentence in German using information from the dialogue.

Susan Bell

Dieter Pohl

Herr Nowakowski

Otto Hinze

Mann:	**Hallo, Herr Pohl. Wie geht's?**
Herr Pohl:	**Recht gut, danke. Und Ihnen?**
Mann:	**Ausgezeichnet, danke. Darf ich vorstellen: Susan Bell, das ist Dieter Pohl.**
Frau Bell:	**Guten Tag, Herr Pohl.**
Herr Pohl:	**Guten Tag, Frau Bell. Freut mich. Kommen Sie aus den USA?**
Frau Bell:	**Ja, aus New York. Und Sie? Sind Sie von hier?**
Herr Pohl:	**Nein, ich bin nicht aus Köln. Ich komme aus Wien.**

Mann:	**Ist das Monsieur Borsart aus Paris?**
Frau:	**Nein, das ist Herr Nowakowski aus Polen.**

Frau Dittrich:	**Herr Walter?**
Herr Walter:	**Ja?**
Frau Dittrich:	**Guten Tag. Ich bin Erika Dittrich, und das ist Otto Hinze aus Bern.**
Herr Hinze:	**Guten Tag.**
Herr Walter:	**Freut mich.**

Sein "to Be"

The verb *sein* "to be" is an irregular verb, like in English. It's also a very useful verb. Here are the forms of the present tense:

ich	bin	I	am
Sie	sind	you	are (s./pl., for.)
du	bist	you	are (s., inf.)
er/sie/es	ist	he/she/it	is
wir	sind	we	are
ihr	seid	you	are (pl., inf.)
sie	sind	they	are

5. LISTENING ACTIVITY

Now listen to the pronunciation of several country names in German. Can you say them like a native?

Australien	Australia
die Vereinigten Staaten	the United States
England	England
Großbritannien	Great Britain
Irland	Ireland
Kanada	Canada
Neuseeland	New Zealand
Nordirland	Northern Ireland
Schottland	Scotland
Südafrika	South Africa
Wales	Wales

6. SPEAKING ACTIVITY

Now put the different elements that you have learned together. Imagine you and a friend are on a plane to Germany. You're sitting next to some German speakers and one of them starts a conversation with you. Make up dialogues using *kommen*, *sein* and other vocabulary from this lesson following the model.

Regina Janssen: **Guten Tag. Ich bin Regina Janssen.**

Sie: **Guten Tag. Ich bin** (name) **und das ist** (friend's name)**.**

Regina Janssen: **Ich komme aus Hamburg. Ich bin auf Geschäftsreise und Sie?**

Sie: **Wir kommen aus** (location)**. Wir sind im Urlaub.**

7. LISTENING ACTIVITY

Listen to the numbers 11-20. Practice pronouncing the numbers like the speaker.

11	elf	14	vierzehn	17	siebzehn	20	zwanzig
12	zwölf	15	fünfzehn	18	achtzehn		
13	dreizehn	16	sechzehn	19	neunzehn		

8. LISTENING ACTIVITY

Can you do simple addition equations with the numbers 1-20 in German?
Listen to the speaker and write out the equations in words.

1 **2 + 4 = 6**

2 **5 – 2 = 3**

3 **7 + 5 = 12**

4 **18 – 8 = 10**

5 **20 – 7 = 13**

6 **17 – 8 = 9**

9. **LISTENING ACTIVITY**

 Pay attention to these flight announcements. What flight numbers and destinations do you hear mentioned? Write them down on the departures board.

Fluggesellschaft	Flugnummer	Ziel	Flugsteig
AA			10
BA			2
QA			7
LH			15
AF			9
LH			12

Letzter Aufruf für American Airlines, Flugnummer AA ... nach ..., Flugsteig 10.
Last call for American Airlines, flight number AA ... to ..., gate 10.

Letzter Aufruf British Airways, Flugnummer BA ... nach ..., Flugsteig 2.
Last call for British Airways, flight number BA ... to ..., gate 2.

Passagiere for Qantas, Flugnummer QA ... nach ..., Flugsteig 7.
Passengers for Qantas, flight number QA ... to ..., gate 7.

Passagiere für Lufthansa, Flugnummer LH ... nach ..., Flugsteig 15.
Passengers for Lufthansa, flight number LH ... to ..., gate 15.

Passagiere für Air France, Flugnummer AF ... nach ...: Dieser Flug hat 20 Minuten Verspätung.
Passengers for Air France, flight number AF ... to ...: your flight is delayed by 20 minutes.

Passagiere für Lufthansa, Flugnummer LH ... nach ..., Flugsteig 12.
Passengers for Lufthansa, flight number LH ... to ..., gate 12.

PRONUNCIATION

 There are five vowels in German: *a, e, i, o* and *u*. These can be pronounced short or long. Listen to the audio to hear the correct pronunciation of these vowel sounds, and practice saying them aloud.

Short Vowels

a	*kann*	can
e	*nett*	nice
i	*ist*	is
o	*kommt*	comes
u	*plus*	plus

Long Vowels

a	*Tag*	day
e	*geht**	goes
i	*wie**	how
o	*so*	so
u	*gut*	good

* In some words, the long vowels are spelled *ah, eh, ie(h), oh, uh*.

Now repeat these pairs of words, one with a short vowel and the other with a long vowel. Really concentrate on making those vowels short or long.

kann, Tag
nett, geht
ist, wie
kommt, so
plus, gut

LEARNING TIP

Don't try to do too much at one time. It is generally better to study for short periods every day and review often than to try to do a whole unit at one sitting. Try to fix a regular time to study: find the best time of day, and always study at that time.

Check It!

Test what you've learned in this lesson and review anything you're not sure of.

CAN YOU . . . ?

- [ ] **ask where someone is from**
  Woher kommen Sie?

- [ ] **say where you're from**
  Ich komme aus …

- [ ] **introduce a friend**
  Das ist …

- [ ] **say that you are on a business trip or on vacation**
  Ich bin auf Geschäftsreise/im Urlaub.

- [ ] **count from 0 to 20**
  null, eins, zwei …

- [ ] **do simple arithmetic**
  Zwei plus vier ist sechs.

Learn More

Search the internet for German language newspapers and go to the foreign news section. Scan the headlines and articles and see how many country names you recognize.

BERLITZ HOTSPOT Go to www.berlitzhotspot.com for…

Social Networking
Share your thoughts on German sounds with your Hotspot friends. Are any of them confusing or challenging for you? Do you have any funny pronunciation stories?

Podcast 3
I'd Like You to Meet…
Download the podcast.

Internet Activity
Would you like to learn more about the geography of German-speaking countries? Go to **Berlitz Hotspot** for links to several maps. Practice making sentences using some of the place names and the verb *kommen*, like *Helen kommt aus Hamburg*.

Video 2– A Business Call
A businesswoman calls an office. What does she say to the receptionist who answers the phone? How does the businesswoman leave a message? Watch the video and learn how to make a business call in German.

Lesson 4 — I'd Like a Coffee, Please.

Einen Kaffee, bitte.

LESSON OBJECTIVES

Lesson 4 is about ordering in a restaurant. When you have completed this lesson, you'll know how to:

- order food and drink
- count by tens
- ask for prices

DIALOGUE

 Listen to this Customer ordering at an *Imbiss*, a snack stand:

Bitte schön?

Yes, please?

Ich möchte eine Bratwurst mit Brot.

I'd like a grilled sausage with bread.

Sonst noch etwas?

Anything else?

Ja, eine Cola.

Yes, a cola, please.

Noch etwas?

Anything else?

Nein, danke.

No, thanks.

Use the following words and expressions to guide you through the lesson.

VOCABULARY

alles	everything	**der Imbiss**	snack bar
das Bier	beer	**der Kaffee**	coffee
bitte	please	**das Käsebrot**	cheese sandwich or roll
Bitte schön?	Yes, please? (i.e., What would you like?)	**klein**	small
		mit	with
die Bratwurst	German grilled sausage	**die Pommes (frites) (pl.)**	French fries
das Brot	bread	**die Portion**	portion
Das ist alles.	That's all.	**das Salamibrot**	salami sandwich or roll
die Cola	cola		
die Currywurst	curried sausage	**der Senf**	mustard
der Euro	euro	**(Sonst) noch etwas?**	Anything else?
groß	big		
ich möchte …	I would like…		

1. DIALOGUE ACTIVITY

What does the customer order?

DID YOU KNOW?

In Germany, the currency symbol is written after the price, and the decimal point is replaced by a comma. So, you'll see, for example, *1,50 €*, which would be read *ein Euro fünfzig* or *eins fünfzig*.

2. LISTENING ACTIVITY

Listen to the dialogue again, then fill in the gaps missing in the conversation with words from the box.

| bitte | Bratwurst | danke | eine Cola | möchte | sonst |

Verkäufer: [_____] schön?

Kundin: Ich [_____] eine [_____] mit Brot.

Verkäufer: [_____] noch etwas?

Kundin: Ja, [_____] [_____].

Verkäufer: Noch etwas?

Kundin: Nein, [_____].

3. SPEAKING ACTIVITY

Have a look at the menu.
Practice reading the items and their prices aloud.

Schnellimbiss
Am Zoo

Bratwurst mit Brot..... 2,50€
Currywurst..... 3,00€
Pommes frites..... 1,70€
Käsebrot..... 2,80€
Salamibrot..... 2,00€
Bier, klein..... 1,90€
Bier, groß..... 2,50€
Kaffee..... 1,70€
Cola..... 2,50€

4. SPEAKING ACTIVITY

 Now try ordering a meal for yourself and a friend. Follow the prompts and order from the menu.

Verkäufer: **Bitte schön?**

Sie: Say that you'd like a fried sausage with bread and a curried sausage.

Verkäufer: **Sonst noch etwas?**

Sie: Say: Yes, one order of French fries.

Verkäufer: **Noch etwas?**

Sie: Say: No, thanks.

Gender of Nouns   GRAMMAR

Nouns in German have one of three genders: masculine, feminine or neuter. The words for "the" and "a" (the articles) change according to the gender of the noun. For example:

	definite article "the"	indefinite article "a"
Masculine:	*der Kaffee*	*ein Kaffee*
Feminine:	*die Wurst*	*eine Wurst*
Neuter:	*das Brot*	*ein Brot*

Note that the definite article is *die* for all nouns in the plural, regardless of gender: *die Pommes frites.*

Ein/Eine, "a" or "one", has no direct plural.

There is no particular logic as to whether a noun is masculine, feminine, or neuter—although there are some clues that we'll be looking at later. You simply have to learn the gender with the noun. For this reason, it's best to learn the noun with its definite article: not *Brot* but *das Brot.* From now on, all the nouns in Vocabulary will be shown with their definite article.

5. SPEAKING ACTIVITY **"99**

Look again at the menu. Use the prices given to identify the item ordered by each customer. Then, fill in the gaps below. Pay attention to your use of *ein/eine*. Look back at the grammar section if you are confused.

Verkäufer: **Bitte schön?**

Kunde 1: _____ , bitte.
Verkäufer: **Drei Euro, bitte.**

Verkäufer: **Bitte schön?**

Kunde 2: _____ , bitte.
Verkäufer: **Ein Euro neunzig, bitte.**

Verkäufer: **Bitte schön?**

Kunde 3: _____ , bitte.
Verkäufer: **Zwei Euro achtzig, bitte.**

Verkäufer: **Bitte schön?**

Kunde 4: _____ , bitte.
Verkäufer: **Zwei Euro fünfzig, bitte.**

Schnellimbiss
Am Zoo

Bratwurst mit Brot..... 2,50€
Currywurst..... 3,00€
Pommes frites..... 1,70€
Käsebrot..... 2,80€
Salamibrot..... 2,00€
Bier, klein..... 1,90€
Bier, groß..... 2,50€
Kaffee..... 1,70€
Cola..... 2,50€

6. LISTENING ACTIVITY

Listen to the numbers 10 to 100. Say them aloud to yourself, concentrating on your pronunciation.

10	zehn	40	vierzig	70	siebzig	100	(ein)hundert
20	zwanzig	50	fünfzig	80	achtzig		
30	dreißig	60	sechzig	90	neunzig		

7. SPEAKING ACTIVITY

 Circle the prices that you hear. Then read aloud the prices that you have circled.

1. 20,01 €	1,20 €	12,– €
2. 3,15 €	50,03 €	3,50 €
3. 18,– €	80,– €	8,– €
4. 8,– €	18,– €	80,– €
5. 30,– €	13,– €	20,– €
6. 30,10 €	13,13 €	13,10 €
7. 50,40 €	40,50 €	14,15 €
8. 7,10 €	70,– €	17,– €
9. 7,70 €	17,70 €	70,70 €
10. 9,90 €	90,09 €	9,10 €

DID YOU KNOW?

Did you notice the use of commas and periods in German prices? A comma is used to separate the decimals, for example, one euro and fifty cents is written *1,50 €*. The period is used to make large numbers readable; amounts that have more than three digits get a period after every third digit, counting from the last one. So a German million looks like this: *1.000.000,00 €*. When the decimal is *00* the two digits are often replaced with a dash, as in *5,– €*.

Check It!

Test what you've learned in this lesson and review anything you're not sure of.

CAN YOU . . . ?

☐ **order food and drink in a café or snack bar**
Ich möchte gern eine Bratwurst.
Eine Bratwurst, bitte.
Ich möchte gern einen Kaffee.
Einen Kaffee, bitte.
Ich möchte gern ein großes Bier.
Ein großes Bier, bitte.

☐ **say that's all**
Das ist alles.

☐ **count by tens**
zehn, zwanzig, dreißig …

 BERLITZ HOTSPOT Go to www.berlitzhotspot.com for…

Social Networking
Have you had any funny experiences in German or other foreign restaurants? Tell your Hotspot friends about them.

Podcast 4
Oh, Did You Want to Order Something?
Download the podcast

Internet Activity
Do you like German food? Go to **Berlitz Hotspot** for links to some German restaurants. Have a look at the sites and try ordering some dishes that sound interesting to you.

Video 3 – **Ordering at a Restaurant**
A man orders food at a German restaurant. What does the waitress ask him? How does he respond? Watch the video and learn how to place a food and drink order.

Lesson 5 A Beer, Please!

Ein Bier, bitte!

LESSON OBJECTIVES

Lesson 5 is about ordering drinks. When you have completed this lesson, you'll know how to:

- catch the waiter's attention
- order drinks
- ask for the check

47

DIALOGUE

Here are some customers in a café. Listen as they order.

Table 1

Kellnerin:	**Möchten Sie bestellen?** Are you ready to order?
Gast:	**Ja, ich möchte einen Tee, bitte.** Yes, I'd like a tea, please.
Kellnerin:	**Ceylon oder Earl Grey?** Ceylon or Earl Grey?
Gast:	**Ceylon, bitte.** Ceylon, please.
Kellnerin:	**Mit Milch oder mit Zitrone?** With milk or lemon?
Gast:	**Mit Zitrone.** With lemon.

Table 2

Kellner:	**Was darf es sein?** What would you like?
Gast:	**Ich möchte einen Kaffee, bitte.** I'd like a coffee, please.
Kellner:	**Espresso, Cappuccino oder Filter?** Espresso, cappuccino or (drip) coffee?
Gast:	**Einen Filterkaffee.** A (drip) coffee, please.
Kellner:	**Sonst noch etwas?** Anything else?
Gast:	**Nein, danke.** No, thanks.

Table 3

Kellnerin:	**Was darf es sein?** What would you like?
Gast:	**Ein Bier, bitte.** A beer, please.
Kellnerin:	**Ein Pils oder ein Export?** A pilsner beer or an export beer?
Gast:	**Ein Pils, bitte.** A pilsner beer, please.
Kellnerin:	**Ein kleines oder ein großes?** A small one or a large one?
Gast:	**Ein großes.** A large one.

Table 4

Kellner:	**Guten Tag. Sie wünschen?** Hello. What can I get you?
Gast:	**Haben Sie Fruchtsaft?** Do you have fruit juice?
Kellner:	**Ja, natürlich. Wir haben Orangensaft, Grapefruitsaft, Apfelsaft …** Yes, sure. We have orange juice, grapefruit juice, apple juice…
Gast:	**Ich möchte einen Orangensaft, bitte.** I'd like an orange juice, please.

Use the following words and expressions to
guide you through the lesson.

VOCABULARY

also	well	**kalt**	cold
der Apfelsaft	apple juice	**das Kännchen**	pot (of tea or coffee)
die Apfelschorle	apple juice and mineral water	**die Milch**	milk
die Bedienung	service, waitress	**Mit Milch oder mit Zitrone?**	With milk or with lemon?
die Berliner Weiße	light beer with red or green syrup	**oder**	or
bestellen	to order	**der Orangensaft**	orange juice
der Cappuccino	cappuccino	**das Pils**	pilsner beer (a pale lager)
der Espresso	espresso		
das Export	export beer (a dark beer)	**die Rechnung**	check (bill)
		die Sahne	cream
der Fruchtsaft	fruit juice	**die Sahnehaube**	whipped cream topping
für	for		
das Glas	glass	**die Schokolade**	chocolate
der Grapefruitsaft	grapefruit juice	**die Speisekarte**	menu
heiß	hot	**still (ohne Kohlensäure)**	still (non-carbonated)
die heiße Schokolade	hot chocolate	**der Tee**	tea
Herr Ober!	Waiter!	**was**	what
Ich hätte gern ...	I would like…	**wünschen**	want, wish
Ich möchte ...	I would like… (less formal)	**(be)zahlen**	pay
der Kaffee	coffee	**die Zitrone**	lemon

1. DIALOGUE ACTIVITY

What does each customer order?

49

2. SPEAKING ACTIVITY

Now that you've found a promising café and a nice table with a good view, you need to get some service. Practice saying these useful restaurant phrases aloud.

Sie: **Hallo!/Entschuldigung!** Hello!/Excuse me!

Sie: **Die Speisekarte, bitte.** The menu, please.

Kellner: **Was darf es sein?/Möchten Sie bestellen?/Sie wünschen?** What would you like?

Sie: **Zahlen, bitte./Die Rechnung, bitte.** Pay, please./The check, please.

3. ACTIVITY

Match the most appropriate caption to each of the pictures below.

A. **Entschuldigung! Die Speisekarte bitte!**

B. **Was darf es sein?**

C. **Ich möchte bitte bestellen!**

D. **Ich möchte bitte bezahlen!**

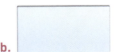  

a.   b.   c.   d.

4. LISTENING ACTIVITY

Now, listen to some more people ordering drinks in a café. Imagine you are the waiter; note what each table wants to order.

5. SPEAKING ACTIVITY

You and your friends are at a café in Frankfurt. Order the following. Then listen to the audio to check your answers.

a. **tea**

b. **coffee**

c. **a beer**

d. **an orange juice**

Masculine Nouns

GRAMMAR

You may have noticed in the last exercise that when you say you would like a cup of coffee *ein Kaffee* becomes *einen Kaffee: Ich möchte einen Kaffee, bitte.*

Why has *ein* become *einen*?

To understand this, you need to know a little about subjects and objects. When you say *Ich möchte einen Kaffee*, the person who wants the coffee, in this case *ich*, is the subject. The coffee is the object, the thing that is wanted. To put it another way, the subject is performing the action; the object is affected by the action.

Now, when a masculine noun becomes the object of a verb, *ein* changes to *einen*. Only the masculine articles change in this way:

Masculine: *ein Kaffee*   *Ich möchte einen Kaffee.*
Feminine: *eine Cola*   *Ich möchte eine Cola.*
Neuter: *ein Brot*   *Ich möchte ein Brot.*

6. WRITING ACTIVITY

Write down how you would order the following items using "I would like," *Ich möchte/Ich hätte gern …* Keep in mind the ideas of subject and object and make any necessary changes to the articles.

1. **der Apfelsaft**

2. **der Cappuccino**

3. **der Espresso**

4. **das Export**

5. **der Fruchtsaft**

6. **das Kännchen**

7. **die Milch**

8. **der Orangensaft**

9. **das Pils**

10. **die heiße Schokolade**

7. **SPEAKING** **ACTIVITY**

Imagine you are at Café Kranzler. Here's part of a menu. Order a pastry and a drink of your choice.

⌘ *Menu* ⌘

Sachertorte	2,80 €
Bienenstich	1,90 €
Streuselkuchen	2,90 €
Spezialität des Hauses	
Kanzlerschnitte	3,00 €
(Schoko-Sahneschnitte mit Ananasgeschmack)	
Tasse Schokolade	2,50 €
Tasse Kaffee	2,20 €
Glas Tee	1,90 €

8. **SPEAKING** **ACTIVITY**

Now let's put everything together. Complete the dialogues with an appropriate response.

Kellnerin: **Möchten Sie bestellen?**

Gast:

Kellnerin: **Espresso, Cappuccino oder Filterkaffee?**

Gast:

Kellnerin: **Das ist alles?**

Gast:

Kellner: **Was darf es sein?**

Gast:

Kellner: **Export, Pils, Berliner Weiße …?**

Gast:

Kellner: **Sonst noch etwas?**

Gast:

Check It!

Test what you've learned in this lesson and review anything you're not sure of.

CAN YOU . . . ?

☐ **attract the waiter's or waitress' attention**
Hallo!
Entschuldigung!

☐ **ask to order**
Ich möchte bitte bestellen.

☐ **ask for the menu**
Die Speisekarte, bitte!

☐ **understand when the waiter asks to take your order**
Was darf es sein?
Möchten Sie bestellen?
Sie wünschen?

☐ **order using *ich hätte gern***

☐ **ask to pay**
Ich möchte bitte bezahlen.

BERLITZ HOTSPOT   Go to www.berlitzhotspot.com for...

Social Networking
Chat with your Hotspot friends about you favorite German food or drinks. Then, tell your Hotspot friends about any exotic German food you would like to try. You may need to do some research first!

Podcast 5
Ein Bier, bitte.
Download the podcast.

Internet Activity
Visit the websites of the German restaurants from Lesson 4. Review the menus, write down a list of what you'd like to order, and then practice ordering aloud. If you're not sure what some of the items on the menus are, use a bilingual dictionary.

Lesson 6 | At the Market

Auf dem Markt

LESSON OBJECTIVES

Lesson 6 is about buying in a market. When you have completed this lesson, you'll know how to:

- ask for items and specific weights of items
- count to 1000

DIALOGUE

 Listen to two customers making purchases at Winterfeldplatz outdoor market in Berlin.

1

Kunde:	**Was kosten die Rosen?**
	How much are the roses?
Verkäuferin:	**Eine kostet 2 €.**
	2 € a piece.
Kunde:	**Mmhhhh, sie duften so gut! Ich nehme sechs.**
	Mmhhhh, they smell lovely! I'll take six.

2

Kundin:	**Guten Tag. Haben Sie Vollkornbrot?**
	Hello. Do you have whole wheat bread?
Verkäuferin:	**Ja.**
	Yes, we do.
Kundin:	**Ich möchte ein großes, bitte.**
	I'd like a large one, please.
Verkäuferin:	**Sonst noch etwas?**
	Anything else?
Kundin:	**Das ist alles.**
	That's all.
Verkäuferin:	**3,40 €, bitte.**
	3.40 €, please.

1. DIALOGUE ACTIVITY

A. What does each customer ask for?

B. What does each customer purchase?

Use the following words and expressions to guide you through the lesson.

VOCABULARY

aber	but	**nehmen**	to take
die Ansichtskarte (-n)	postcard	**die Nelke (-n)**	carnation
		das Obst	fruit
die Bäckerei (-en)	bakery	**die Olive (-n)**	olive
billig	cheap	**die Orange (-n)**	orange
bitte schön	here you are	**probieren**	to try
dann	then, in that case	**die Rose (-n)**	rose
diese	these	**der Schafskäse**	sheep's milk cheese
Es schmeckt gut!	It tastes good!		
ganz	very, completely	**schwarz**	black
das Gemüse	vegetable(s)	**Sehen Sie?**	You see?
das Gramm (-)	gram	**Sie duften so gut!**	They smell so nice!
groß	big	**das Souvenir (-s)**	souvenir
haben	to have	**süß**	sweet
insgesamt	altogether	**Vier Stück, bitte.**	Four (pieces), please.
der Käse (-)	cheese		
kosten	to cost	**das Vollkornbrot (-e)**	whole wheat bread
lecker	delicious	**Was kostet es?**	How much is it?

DID YOU KNOW?

Did you notice the plural endings were included in parentheses, above? Add an *e* to the end of the word to form the plural when you see (-e). So if you are talking about more than one whole wheat bread, *das Vollkornbrot* changes to *die Vollkornbrote*. Add *en* if (-en) is given in parentheses: *die Bäckerei*, (bakery) = *die Bäckereien* (bakeries). When you see (¨) a vowel changes to an *Umlaut*: *der Apfel* (apple) = *die Äpfel* (apples) when you are using the plural form (note that the position of the *Umlaut* may vary, based on the number of syllables in the word). The dash (-) alone means that the noun doesn't change in the plural: *das Gemüse* (vegetable/vegetables).

2. LISTENING ACTIVITY

Listen to the conversations from before as well as some other people buying items in the market. Which conversation belongs to each of these market stalls?

1

Kunde:	**Was kosten die Rosen?** How much are the roses?
Verkäuferin:	**Eine kostet 2 €.** 2 € a piece.
Kunde:	**Mmhhhh, sie duften so gut! Ich nehme sechs.** Mmhhhh, they smell lovely! I'll take six.

2

Kundin:	**Guten Tag. Haben Sie Vollkornbrot?** Hello. Do you have whole wheat bread?
Verkäuferin:	**Ja.** Yes, we do.
Kundin:	**Ich möchte ein großes, bitte.** I'd like a large one, please.
Verkäuferin:	**Sonst noch etwas?** Anything else?
Kundin:	**Das ist alles.** That's all.
Verkäuferin:	**3,40 €, bitte.** 3.40 €, please.

3

Kunde: **Tag. Was kosten die Ansichtskarten?** Hi. How much are the postcards?

Verkäuferin: **75 Cent.** 0.75 €.

Kunde: **Dann nehme ich drei.** OK, I'll take three.

4

Kunde: **Guten Morgen.** Good morning.

Verkäuferin: **Guten Morgen.** Good morning.

Kunde: **Haben Sie Schafskäse?** Do you have feta cheese?

Verkäuferin: **Ja natürlich.** Yes, of course.

Kunde: **Ich möchte zweihundert Gramm, bitte.** I'd like two hundred grams, please.

Verkäuferin: **Bitte schön.** Here you are.

5

Kundin: **Guten Tag. Sind die Orangen süß?** Hi. Are the oranges sweet?

Verkäufer: **Ja, süß und ganz frisch.** Yes, they're sweet and really fresh.

Kundin: **Dann nehme ich fünf Stück.** OK, I'll take five.

3. SPEAKING ACTIVITY

 Practice more useful expressions for buying things. *Haben Sie ...*

 Haben Sie ... Do you have...

Haben Sie Vollkornbrot? Do you have whole wheat bread?

 Was kostet es? How much does it cost?

 Was kosten sie? How much do they cost?

 Darf ich probieren? May I try?

4. SPEAKING ACTIVITY

You're going shopping at the market. Here's your list of things to buy.

400 g Edamer Käse
5 Nektarinen
5 Orangen
100 g schwarze Oliven

To get you started, here's the first dialogue, with space for you to complete your responses:

Verkäufer: **Guten Tag! Sie wünschen?**

Sie:

Say hello, and ask if he has Edam cheese.

Verkäufer: **Aber natürlich! Hundert Gramm für neunzig Cent.**

Sie:

Say you'll take four hundred grams.

Verkäufer: **Bitte schön. Sonst noch etwas?**

Sie:

Say: No, thanks.

Verkäufer: **Drei Euro sechzig, bitte.**

Now try to make the remaining purchases without preparing written notes.

5. WRITING ACTIVITY

Here are the numbers 20–24. Can you complete writing the numbers up to forty?
The pattern is completely regular.

20 **zwanzig**	27	34
21 **einundzwanzig**	28	35
22 **zweiundzwanzig**	29	36

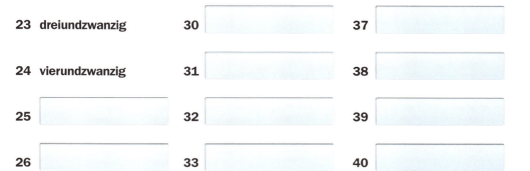

23 dreiundzwanzig	**30**	**37**	
24 vierundzwanzig	**31**	**38**	
25	**32**	**39**	
26	**33**	**40**	

6. LISTENING ACTIVITY

Circle the number you hear from each pair:

a. 34   43
b. 13   30
c. 97   79
d. 35   53
e. 82   28
f. 62   26
g. 39   93
h. 80   18
i. 41   51
j. 56   65

7. LISTENING ACTIVITY

 Listen to the pronunciation of the numbers by hundreds up to 1000, then say the numbers aloud, attempting to imitate the speaker as closely as you can.

100	(ein)hundert	500	fünfhundert	900	neunhundert
200	zweihundert	600	sechshundert	1000	(ein)tausend
300	dreihundert	700	siebenhundert		
400	vierhundert	800	achthundert		

PRONUNCIATION

 Remember that vowels with the *Umlaut*, ¨, are pronounced differently than those without the mark.

How would you pronounce these words? Try saying them aloud, then listen to the audio to check your pronunciation.

Tag	day	*Käse*	cheese
schon	already	*schön*	beautiful
gut	good	*Stück*	piece

Plural Nouns

Not many German nouns form their plurals with an *-s* like English nouns (these are usually words taken from English and French: e.g., *das Souvenir, die Souvenirs*). Feminine nouns ending in *-e* in the singular always take *-n* in the plural:

die Rose	the rose
die Rosen	the roses

You'll come across other plural forms in the following units.

LEARNING TIP

Be selective in your vocabulary learning. Don't feel that you have to learn every word and expression you find in this course. Instead, choose the 15–20 words or expressions from each spread that seem most useful and relevant to you, and aim to make them stick in your memory. That way, by the end of the course you'll have an active German vocabulary of between 540 and 720 words. But you'll also find that you've absorbed a much larger passive vocabulary through hearing and reading lots of German.

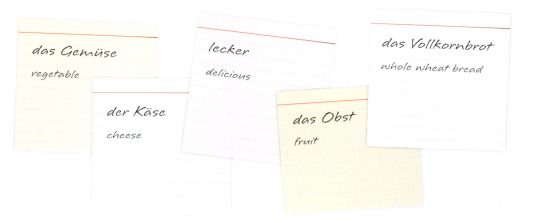

das Gemüse
vegetable

lecker
delicious

das Vollkornbrot
whole wheat bread

der Käse
cheese

das Obst
fruit

Check It!

Test what you've learned in this lesson and review anything you're not sure of.

CAN YOU . . . ?

☐ **count by hundreds to 1000**
hundert, zweihundert, ..., tausend

☐ **ask about availability of an item**
Haben Sie Fruchtsaft?
Haben Sie Käse?

☐ **ask for a specific weight of an item**
Vierhundert Gramm Käse, bitte.

Learn More

If someone you know is going to a German-speaking country, ask him/her to bring back magazines with cooking recipes and checks from restaurants and cafés. Some restaurants and cafés may let you take a menu. See how many names of foods and drinks you can identify, and practice ordering them.

BERLITZ HOTSPOT   Go to www.berlitzhotspot.com for...

Social Networking
If you've traveled to German-speaking countries, share which specialty stores you had to go to purchase items you wanted with your Hotspot friends. Or, tell them which stores you plan on visiting!

Podcast 6
How.Much Is That?
Download the podcast.

Internet Activity
Go to **Berlitz Hotspot** for links to some large German stores on the internet and access their current catalogues. Flip through and see how many items you can identify.

Video 4 – Making a Purchase
A woman makes a purchase at a cheese shop. What does she ask the gentleman behind the counter? How much does the cheese cost? Watch the video and learn how to request and buy items in a German shop.

Lesson 7 | This Is My Family.

Das ist meine Familie.

LESSON OBJECTIVES

Lesson 7 is about family life. When you have completed this lesson, you'll know how to:

- state your marital status
- describe family relationships
- introduce family members

DIALOGUE

 Here are some people answering the question: *Sind Sie verheiratet?*
(Are you married?)

Frau 1:	**Sind Sie verheiratet?**	Are you married?
Frau 2:	**Ja, ich bin verheiratet.**	Yes, I'm married.

Frau 1:	**Sind Sie verheiratet?**	Are you married?
Mann 1:	**Nein, ich bin noch ledig.**	No, I'm still single.

Frau 1:	**Sind Sie verheiratet?**	Are you married?
Mann 2:	**Nein, ich bin geschieden.**	No, I'm divorced.

Frau 1:	**Und sind Sie verheiratet?**	And are you married?
Frau 2:	**Nein, aber ich habe einen Partner.**	No, but I have a partner.

Frau 1:	**Sind Sie verheiratet?**	Are you married?
Mann 3:	**Ja, aber wir leben getrennt.**	Yes, but we're separated.

1. DIALOGUE ACTIVITY

What are some different ways to describe one's marital status?

Use the following words and expressions to
guide you through the lesson.

VOCABULARY

aber	but	**das Kind (-er)**	child
die Beziehung (-en)	relationship	**klein**	small
der Bruder (¨)	brother	**leben**	to live
die Eltern	parents	**ledig**	single, unmarried
das Enkelkind (-er)	grandchild	**leider**	unfortunately
der Enkelsohn (-söhne)	grandson	**der Mann (¨-er)**	husband, man
		mein/e	my
die Enkeltochter (-töchter)	granddaughter	**die Mutter (¨)**	mother
die Familie (-n)	family	**noch**	still
die Frau (-en)	wife, Mrs., woman	**noch nicht**	not yet
geschieden	divorced	**der Onkel (-)**	uncle
die Geschwister	brothers and sisters, siblings	**der Partner (-)**	partner (male)
		die Partnerin (-nen)	partner (female)
getrennt	separated	**die Schwester (-n)**	sister
die Großmutter (-mütter)	grandmother	**der Sohn (¨-e)**	son
		die Tante (-n)	aunt
der Großvater (-väter)	grandfather	**die Tochter (¨)**	daughter
haben	to have	**der Vater (¨)**	father
Ihr/e	your (for.)	**verheiratet**	married
jung	young	**zu**	too, to
kein/e	none, not any		

2. LISTENING ACTIVITY

Listen to six different speakers. How many sons and daughters does each have? Write the number in the space provided.

Sohn/Söhne	Tochter/Töchter

1

Frau 1:   **Haben Sie Kinder?**

Mann 1:   **Ja, ich habe eine Tochter.**

2

Frau 1:   **Haben Sie Kinder?**

Frau 2:   **Ja, wir haben einen Sohn.**

3

Frau 1:   **Haben Sie Kinder?**

Frau 3:   **Ja, ich habe zwei Söhne, Ralf und Matthias.**

4

Frau 1:   **Haben Sie Kinder?**

Mann 2:   **Nein, noch nicht.**

5

Frau 1:   **Haben Sie Kinder?**

Mann 3:   **Ja, ich habe drei Kinder: einen Sohn und zwei Töchter.**

6

Frau 1:   **Und haben Sie Kinder?**

Frau 4:   **Nein, leider noch nicht.**

Haben, to Have — GRAMMAR

Haben is an irregular verb. You'll need it often, so it's worth memorizing:

ich	habe	I	have
Sie	haben	you	have (sg./pl., for.)
du	hast	you	have (sg., inf.)
er/sie/es	hat	he/she/it	has
wir	haben	we	have
ihr	habt	you	have (pl., inf.)
sie	haben	they	have

3. SPEAKING ACTIVITY

 Fill in the information to complete Anna Wieland's family tree below. Listen to the audio to hear the terms for family members.

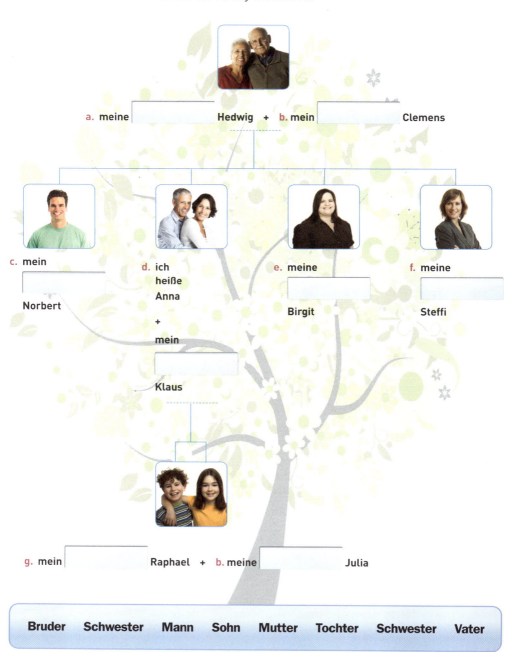

a. meine [____] Hedwig + b. mein [____] Clemens

c. mein [____] Norbert

d. ich heiße Anna + mein [____] Klaus

e. meine [____] Birgit

f. meine [____] Steffi

g. mein [____] Raphael + b. meine [____] Julia

Bruder   Schwester   Mann   Sohn   Mutter   Tochter   Schwester   Vater

4. SPEAKING ACTIVITY 66 99

Using Anna's family tree, complete the following statements with the correct form of *haben*. If the subject is *ich/wir,* the speaker's name appears before the statement.

1. (Hedwig) Ich [_____] vier Kinder.

2. Anna [_____] zwei Schwestern.

3. (Anna und Klaus) Wir [_____] einen Sohn.

4. Hedwig und Clemens [_____] zwei Enkelkinder.

5. Anna, [_____] Sie einen Bruder?

Nominative and Accusative Cases   GRAMMAR

Remember: In *Ich habe einen Bruder,* "I have a brother", *ich* is the subject, the one who "has"; *Bruder* is the object, the one who is "had," and so it's *einen Bruder.* (The subject of a sentence is said to be "in the nominative case" and the object is here "in the accusative case.")

Possessive Adjectives

The possessive adjectives are: *mein* "my," *unser* "our," *Ihr* "your," *sein* "his, its," and *ihr,* "her, their." They take the same endings as the indefinite article *ein*:

Das ist mein/unser/Ihr/sein/ihr Bruder.
Das ist meine/unsere/Ihre/seine/ihre Schwester.
Das ist mein/unser/Ihr/sein/ihr Kind.

If they refer to a plural noun, they take the ending *-e*:
Das sind meine/unsere/Ihre/seine/ihre Brüder (Schwestern/Kinder).

Not any, *kein*
Kein is the negative of *ein,* as in *Ich habe keinen Bruder,* "I don't have a brother." (*Ich habe nicht einen Bruder* is incorrect German.)
Kein takes the same endings as the possessive adjectives.

5. WRITING ACTIVITY

You are provided a series of nouns. Write the possessive adjective for each and then write the translation, following the example.

ICH

mein	Partner	my partner
	Familie	
	Mutter	
	Enkelkinder	

WIR

	Brüder	
	Geschwister	
	Großmutter	
	Kind	

IHR

	Frauen	
	Männer	
	Schwester	
	Vater	

SIE

	Eltern	
	Sohn	
	Tochter	
	Großvater	

6. SPEAKING ACTIVITY

Make a family tree for yourself and talk about your (extended) family using the verb *haben* as well as possessive adjectives. Make statements like: "I have two brothers and one sister" or "I have no children". Can you also give at least one detail about everyone: first and last name, location, etc.?

7. WRITING ACTIVITY

Answer these questions about the members of Frau Wieland's family. Use *ihr/ihre*, "her," instead of Frau Wieland, as in the example. Remember that you have to use *ihr* for masculine and *ihre* for feminine family members.

Example:

Heißt Frau Wielands Bruder Richard?
Nein, ihr Bruder heißt Norbert.

a.
Heißen Frau Wielands Eltern Julia und Raphael?

b.
Heißen Frau Wielands Schwestern Anna und Steffi?

c.
Wie heißt Frau Wielands Tochter?

d.
Heißt Frau Wielands Mann Klaus?

e.
Heißt Frau Wielands Sohn Norbert?

Check It!

Test what you've learned in this lesson and review anything you're not sure of.

CAN YOU . . . ?

state your marital status
Ich bin verheiratet.
Ich bin ledig.
Ich bin geschieden.

give the names of family members
Mein Vater heißt …
Meine Mutter heißt …

ask someone about his/her marital status
Sind Sie verheiratet?

ask someone about his/her family
Haben Sie Familie?
Wie heißt Ihr Sohn?

list the members of your family
Ich habe einen Bruder.
Ich habe eine Schwester.
Ich habe einen Sohn.
Ich habe eine Tochter.
Ich habe einen Partner.
Ich habe eine Partnerin.

BERLITZ HOTSPOT

Go to www.berlitzhotspot.com for…

Social Networking
Tell your Hotspot friends about you and your family. Do you have brothers or sisters? Do you have children?

Podcast 7
Today's German Family
Download the podcast.

Internet Activity
Search for some family photos on the internet. Make up stories about the people in the pictures, using vocabulary that you have learned in this section. Try to incorporate vocabulary from previous sections as well about where people are from, for example.

Video 5 – My Family
Two friends talk about family relationships. How many siblings does the man have? Who's married? Watch the video and learn how to talk about your family in German.

Lesson 8

What's Your Profession?

Was sind Sie von Beruf?

LESSON OBJECTIVES

Lesson 8 is about work. When you have completed this lesson, you'll know how to:

- talk about your profession
- discuss what others do for a living

DIALOGUE

 Listen to these people talk about where they work.

1

    Frau 1: **Wo arbeiten Sie?** Where do you work?

    Frau 2: **Ich arbeite in einer Bank.** I work in a bank.

2

    Frau 1: **Wo arbeiten Sie?** Where do you work?

    Frau 3: **Ich arbeite in einer Schule.** I work at a school.

3

    Frau 1: **Wo arbeiten Sie?** Where do you work?

    Mann 1: **Ich arbeite in einem Geschäft.** I work in a store.

1. DIALOGUE ACTIVITY

Where does each person work?

Use the following words and expressions to guide you through the lesson.

VOCABULARY

an	at
arbeiten	to work
arbeitslos	unemployed
die Bank (-en)	bank
bei	at, for
der Beruf (-e)	profession
das Büro (-s)	office
die Fabrik (-en)	factory
falsch	false
das Geschäft (-e)	store, business
in	in
das Krankenhaus (-häuser)	hospital
das Restaurant (-s)	restaurant
die Schule (-n)	school
selbstständig	independent(ly), for oneself
die Universität (-en)	university
wahr	true
Was sind Sie von Beruf?	What's your profession?
wo	where
zur Zeit	at the moment

PROFESSIONS

Architekt (-en)/ Architektin (-nen)	architect
Arzt (¨-e)/ Ärztin (-nen)	doctor
Bäcker (-)/ Bäckerin (-nen)	baker
Bauarbeiter (-)/ Bauarbeiterin (-nen)	construction worker
Computertechniker (-)/ Computertechnikerin (-nen)	computer technician
Fotograf (-en)/ Fotografin (-nen)	photographer
Friseur (-e)/ Friseurin (-nen)	hairdresser
Kassierer (-)/ Kassiererin (-nen)	cashier
Kellner (-)/ Kellnerin (-nen)	waiter/waitress
Krankenpfleger (-)/ Krankenpflegerin (-nen)	nurse
Kundenberater (-)/ Kundenberaterin (-nen)	consultant
Künstler (-)/ Künstlerin (-nen)	artist
Lehrer (-)/ Lehrerin (-nen)	teacher
Professor (-en)/ Professorin (-nen)	professor
Regisseur (-e)/ Regisseurin (-nen) (film)	director
Schauspieler (-)/ Schauspielerin (-nen)	actor/actress
Student (-en)/ Studentin (-nen)	student
Taxifahrer (-)/ Taxifahrerin (-nen)	taxi driver
Techniker (-)/ Technikerin (-nen)	technician
Verkäufer (-)/ Verkäuferin (-nen)	sales clerk

2. LISTENING ACTIVITY

Listen to the recording. You will hear five people giving their name and their profession. Fill in their professions on the business cards below. You might refer to the list of professions.

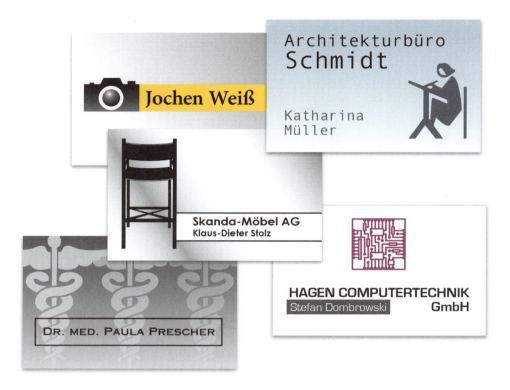

Jochen Weiß

Architekturbüro
Schmidt

Katharina
Müller

Skanda-Möbel AG
Klaus-Dieter Stolz

HAGEN COMPUTERTECHNIK
Stefan Dombrowski   GmbH

Dr. med. Paula Prescher

DID YOU KNOW?

In German a résumé is called *ein Lebenslauf* or *Curriculum Vitae* and typically includes a picture as well as personal information such as date of birth and address. Also, German *Lebensläufe* are dated and signed.

CURRICULUM VITAE

Name: Marianne Kemmerer
Geburtsdatum: 01.01.1986
Geburtsort: Frankfurt am Main
Anschrift: Fröhlichstraße 25,
60311 Frankfurt am Main
Deutschland
Telefon: +49 (0)69 5646124
E-Mail: marianne.kemmerer@mail.de
Studium: 10/2004 – 01/2009
Studium der Betriebswirtschaftslehre
an der Max-Muster-Universität

3. WRITING ACTIVITY

What are the professions of the people below? Write down what they do for a living, then make negative statements.

Dieter Speck

A. **Dieter Speck ist** |_____|.

Er ist kein |_____|.

Sonja Brückner

B. **Sonja Brückner ist** |_____|.

Sie ist keine |_____|.

Rudi Dessau

C. **Rudi Dessau ist** |_____|.

Er ist kein |_____|.

Andreas Freitag

D. **Andreas Freitag ist** |_____|.

Er ist kein |_____|.

| Bauarbeiter | Künstler | Schauspielerin | Friseurin |
| Regisseur | Taxifahrer | Kassierer | Bäcker |

4. LISTENING ACTIVITY

 Listen to six people saying where they work. Match each statement to the corresponding picture.

a. **Ich bin Kassiererin.**

b. **Ich bin Kellner.**

c. **Ich bin Krankenpfleger.**

d. **Ich bin Lehrerin.**

e. **Ich bin Professorin.**

f. **Ich bin Verkäufer.**

1. [   ]

2. [   ]

3. [   ]

4. [   ]

5. [   ]

6. [   ]

Frau 1:	**Wo arbeiten Sie?**
Frau 2:	**Ich arbeite in einer Bank.**
Frau 1:	**Wo arbeiten Sie?**
Frau 3:	**Ich arbeite in einer Schule.**
Frau 1:	**Wo arbeiten Sie?**
Mann 1:	**Ich arbeite in einem Geschäft.**
Frau 1:	**Wo arbeiten Sie?**
Mann 1:	**Ich arbeite in einem Restaurant.**
Frau 1:	**Wo arbeiten Sie?**
Mann 3:	**Ich arbeite in einem Krankenhaus.**
Frau 1:	**Wo arbeiten Sie?**
Frau 4:	**Ich arbeite an der Universität.**

GRAMMAR

Dative Case

Notice that the German for "in a bank" is *in einer Bank*, and "in a store" is *in einem Geschäft*. These are the endings of the dative case. The dative is used after prepositions (words that indicate position) like *in* "in," or *an* "at," when they indicate location, and always after the prepositions *aus* "out of/from" and *von* "from/of."

5. SPEAKING ACTIVITY

When you're asked whether you work in a place, say *Ja, ich bin …* and give a suitable job title, remembering to use the male or female form as appropriate. Here are the questions; you might want to prepare your answers before listening to the recording.

a. **Arbeiten Sie in einem Restaurant?**
b. **Arbeiten Sie in einem Geschäft?**
c. **Arbeiten Sie in einer Schule?**

d. **Arbeiten Sie an der Universität?**
e. **Arbeiten Sie in einer Bank?**
f. **Arbeiten Sie in einem Krankenhaus?**

6. SPEAKING ACTIVITY

Practice saying these expressions aloud. Try to pronounce them as the German speaker does.

Ich arbeite bei …	I work for…
Ich bin selbstständig.	I'm self-employed.
Ich bin zurzeit arbeitslos.	I'm unemployed.
Ich bin Rentner./Ich bin Rentnerin.	I'm retired.
Ich bin Student./Ich bin Studentin.	I'm a student.

7. WRITING ACTIVITY

Answer the following questions about yourself in complete sentences.

1. **Wie heißen Sie?**

2. **Woher kommen Sie?**

3. **Sind Sie verheiratet?**

4. **Was sind Sie von Beruf?**

5. **Wo arbeiten Sie?**

Check It!

Test what you've learned in this lesson and review anything you're not sure of.

CAN YOU . . . ?

☐ **say what you and others do for a living**
Ich bin Architekt/in.
Er ist Taxifahrer.
Sie ist Kassiererin.
Sie sind arbeitslos.

☐ **say where you work**
Ich arbeite in einer Bank/an einer Universität.

BERLITZ HOTSPOT   Go to www.berlitzhotspot.com for...

Social Networking
Tell your Hotspot friends what your profession is and where you work.

Podcast 8
What's Your Profession?
Download the podcast.

Internet Activity
Search for *jobs* on the internet or go to **Berlitz Hotspot** for suggestions. Browse the different lines of work. How many new words can you recognize? Try creating some sentences based with your new vocabulary.

Lesson 9 | You Speak German Well!

Sie sprechen gut Deutsch!

LESSON OBJECTIVES

Lesson 9 is about languages and nationalities. When you have completed this lesson, you'll know how to:

- say which languages you and others speak
- give your nationality and talk about other people's nationalities
- state your age

DIALOGUE

Listen to these people talk about the languages they speak.

Welche Sprachen sprechen Sie?

Which languages do you speak?

Ich spreche Englisch, Französisch und ein bisschen Italienisch.

I speak English, French, and a little Italian.

Und Sie?

And you?

Englisch und Türkisch.

English and Turkish.

Und welche Sprachen sprechen Sie?

And which languages do you speak?

Ich spreche ein bisschen Englisch.

I speak a little English.

Und Sie?

And you?

Ich spreche Russisch und ein wenig Polnisch.

I speak Russian and a little Polish.

Use the following words and expressions to guide you through the lesson.

VOCABULARY

alt	old	das Land ("-er)	country
das Alter	age	die Muttersprache (-n)	native language, mother tongue
außerdem	also		
Deutsch	German	Nr. = die Nummer (-n)	number
Englisch	English		
etwas	a bit, something	die Postleitzahl (-en)/PLZ	zip code
der Familienstand	marital status	die Schweiz	Switzerland
Französisch	French	sprechen	speak
die Fremdsprache (-n)	foreign language	die Staatsangehörigkeit (-en)	nationality
genauso	just as		
genauso gut wie	just as well as	die Straße (-n)	street, road
Ich bin ... Jahre alt.	I'm...years old.	die Türkei	Turkey
Ich wohne jetzt in Berlin.	I live in Berlin now.	wie	as, how
		wohnen	live
das Jahr (-e)	year	der Wohnort (-e)	place of residence (town)
jetzt	now		

1. DIALOGUE ACTIVITY

What are some of the languages you hear mentioned in the dialogue?

2. WRITING ACTIVITY

Can you translate the following languages to English?

Deutsch		Polnisch	
Englisch		**Russisch**	
Französisch		**Spanisch**	
Italienisch		**Türkisch**	

3. SPEAKING ACTIVITY 66 99

Look at the nationalities listed below. Who speaks each of the languages listed in Activity 2? Be careful: Some languages are spoken in more than one country—and in some countries, more than one language is spoken.

Amerikaner/in
Australier/in
Brite/Britin
Deutscher/Deutsche
Franzose/Französin

Italiener/in
Kanadier/in
Österreicher/in
Pole/Polin

Russe/Russin
Schweizer/in
Spanier/in
Türke/Türkin

4. LISTENING ACTIVITY

These application forms were sent to a language school by prospective teachers. Listen to the recording, then fill in the missing details.

Form 1:
Name: Berger
Vorname: Claudia
Straße, Nr.: Mozartstraße 72
PLZ: A 8 0 1 0
Wohnort: Graz
Land:
Staatsangehörigkeit: österreichisch
Muttersprache:
Fremdsprachen:
Alter:
Familienstand:

Form 2:
Name: Dogan
Vorname: Mustafa
Straße, Nr.: Domstraße 90
PLZ: 7 9 0 9 8
Wohnort: Freiburg
Land: Deutschland
Staatsangehörigkeit:
Muttersprache: / Deutsch
Fremdsprachen: , Italienisch
Alter:
Familienstand: verheiratet

Form 3:
Name: Tschumi
Vorname: Hans
Straße, Nr.: Spandauer Straße 110a
PLZ: 1 0 7 8 3
Wohnort: Berlin
Land:
Staatsangehörigkeit:
Muttersprache: Deutsch
Fremdsprachen:
Alter: 31
Familienstand:

Hallo. Ich heiße Claudia Berger. Ich bin Österreicherin. Ich komme aus Graz. Ich spreche Deutsch – natürlich – und etwas Italienisch. Ich bin 25 Jahre alt und ledig.

Hallo. Ich heiße Mustafa Dogan. Ich komme aus Freiburg. Ich bin Türke, aber ich spreche Deutsch. Ich spreche außerdem Englisch und Italienisch. Ich bin 27 Jahre alt und verheiratet.

Hallo. Ich heiße Hans Tschumi. Ich komme aus der Schweiz, aber ich wohne jetzt in Berlin. Deutsch ist meine Muttersprache. Ich spreche auch Englisch und Französisch. Ich bin 31 Jahre alt und geschieden.

5. WRITING ACTIVITY

Write out a form for yourself.

Name:

Vorname:

Straße, Nr.:

PLZ:

Wohnort:

Land:

Staatsangehörigkeit:

Muttersprache:

Fremdsprachen:

Alter:

Familienstand:

6. SPEAKING ACTIVITY

Practice introducing yourself the way the speakers did on the recording for Activity 4. Remember to state:

a.   **your name (*Ich heiße ...*)**

b.   **your nationality (*Ich bin ...*)**

c.   **the town and the country you live in (*Ich komme aus/wohne in ...*)**

d.   **what languages you speak (*Ich spreche ...*)**

e.   **your age (*Ich bin ... Jahre alt.*)**

f.   **your marital status (*Ich bin ...*)**

PRONUNCIATION

Notice that *st* and *sp* are pronounced *sht* and *shp* when they are at the beginning of a word.

Spanisch   *Straße*

S at the beginning of a word and when followed by a vowel is pronounced like "ze" in "zeal".

sie   *sind*

But at the end of a word s is pronounced as in "seal".

aus   *es*

GRAMMAR

Sprechen, to Speak

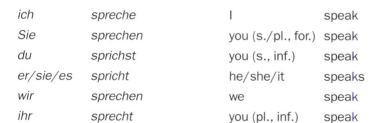

ich	spreche	I	speak
Sie	sprechen	you (s./pl., for.)	speak
du	sprichst	you (s., inf.)	speak
er/sie/es	spricht	he/she/it	speaks
wir	sprechen	we	speak
ihr	sprecht	you (pl., inf.)	speak
sie	sprechen	they	speak

If a verb is irregular in the present tense, it's usually only irregular in the *er/sie/es* form. From now on, we'll just be giving you the irregular forms in the Vocabulary section.

7. WRITING ACTIVITY

Using the prompts, write a sentence using *sprechen*. If the prompt includes a "?", write a question. An example sentence has been done for you.

Example:

(Elsa, Französisch)   *Elsa spricht Französisch.*

1. **(Achim und Helen, Polnisch)**

2. **(Herr Bünchen, Italienisch?)**

3. **(Sandra und ich, Spanisch)**

4. **(Astrid und Bernd, Englisch)**

5. **(Frau Springer, Deutsch?)**

6. **(Florian, Türkisch)**

Feminine Forms of Nationalities   GRAMMAR

The feminine forms of nationalities are generally very easy to form. Like the feminine forms of professions, they add the ending -*in* to the masculine form: *Schweizer/Schweizerin*, "Swiss" (man/woman), etc.

Watch out for these irregular ones:

Brite/Britin	British	*Pole/Polin*	Polish
Deutscher/Deutsche	German	*Russe/Russin*	Russian
Franzose/Französin	French	*Türke/Türkin*	Turkish

8. **WRITING ACTIVITY**

Use vocabulary from this lesson to state information about each person below. Give each person a name and estimate his/her age, state his/her nationality, where he/she comes from and which languages he/she speaks. An example has been done for you.

Example:

Petra ist Deutsche. Sie ist 23 Jahre alt und kommt aus Berlin. Petra spricht Deutsch, Französisch und ein wenig Polnisch.

1.

2.

3.

4.

LEARNING TIP

Try recording your voice when you speak, and listen to the recording to see how you might be able to improve. Record your voice regularly, and keep the recordings. Go back to the beginning of your recording after a few weeks or months to see how you have improved!

Check It!

Test what you've learned
in this lesson and review
anything you're not sure of.

CAN YOU . . . ?

☐ **say what languages you speak**
Ich spreche Deutsch/Englisch/
Französisch.

☐ **give your nationality**
Ich bin Amerikaner/in.
Ich bin Brite/Britin.
Ich bin Deutscher/Deutsche.
Ich bin Schweizer/Schweizerin.
Ich bin Österreicher/Österreicherin.

☐ **state your age**
Ich bin … Jahre alt.

Learn More

Turn to the employment advertisemen
in a German-language newspaper to
see how many of the jobs you recogniz
Use clues from the name of the
company. Guess what the job title
might mean, and then check with
your dictionary.

BERLITZ HOTSPOT   Go to www.berlitzhotspot.com for...

Social Networking
Tell your Hotspot friends your nationality and which languages
are spoken in your area.

Podcast 9
Sprechen Sie Deutsch
Download the podcast

Internet Activity
Search for a German map of the world on the internet.
Make sentences like *Claudia kommt aus Portugal und spricht
Portugiesisch*, which identify people by their nationalities and
the languages they speak.

1. Can you complete the crossword? All the clues are related to food, drink and shopping. Write the answers in capital letters.

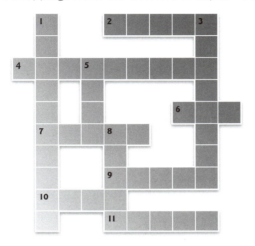

1. **Spicy sausage dish. (10)**

2. **Sechs (pieces) bitte. (5)**

3. **Ich möchte ein** ⬚ **Kaffee. (8)**

4. **Darf ich** ⬚ **? Mmm, es schmeckt gut! (9)**

5. **Alcoholic drink. (4)**

6. ⬚ **nehme vierhundert Gramm von dem Emmentaler. (3)**

7. **Eine Brat** ⬚ **mit Brot, bitte. (5)**

8. **A dairy product. (5)**

9. ⬚ **Sie Orangen? – Ja, natürlich! (5)**

10. **Was darf es** ⬚ **? (4)**

11. **Sonst noch** ⬚ **? (5)**

2. Can you complete these sums?

a. **Achtzehn plus neunzehn ist** [   ]**.**

b. **Einundneunzig minus neunundzwanzig ist** [   ]**.**

c. **Achtundvierzig plus** [   ] **ist siebenundachtzig.**

d. **Hundert minus fünfundvierzig ist** [   ]**.**

e. **Dreizehn plus** [   ] **minus vierundzwanzig ist zwölf.**

3. Complete the sentence with the correct forms of the verbs in parentheses.

a. **Das** [   ] **(sein) Sabine. Sie** [   ]

(kommen) aus Köln. Sie [   ] **(sprechen) Deutsch,**

Englisch und Französisch. Sie [   ] **(sein) verheiratet**

und [   ] **(haben) eine Tochter. Ihre Tochter**

[   ] **(heißen) Jutta.**

b. **Ich** [   ] **(heißen) Klaus. Ich** [   ] **(kommen)**

aus Bremen. Ich [   ] **(sprechen) Englisch und etwas**

Holländisch – und Deutsch, natürlich! Ich [   ] **(sein)**

geschieden und [   ] **(haben) zwei Kinder.**

c. **Ich** [   ] **(sein) Manfred und das** [   ]

(sein) meine Frau Inge. Wir _____ (kommen) beide

aus München. Wir _____ (haben) drei Söhne. Sie

_____ (heißen) Ralf, Jürgen, und Clemens.

4. Can you write sentences following the same pattern as the example?

Example: **Jonathan kommt aus England. Er ist Engländer. Er spricht Englisch.**

a. **Sylvia kommt aus England.**

b. **Bob kommt aus den USA.**

c. **Jasmin kommt aus der Türkei.**

d. **Hans kommt aus Deutschland.**

e. **Isabelle kommt aus Frankreich.**

f. **Marco kommt aus Italien.**

g. **Will kommt aus Australien.**

h. **Mikhail kommt aus Russland.**

i. **Delphine kommt aus der Schweiz. (Französisch)**

j. **Erika kommt aus Österreich.**

5. Look at the family tree, then complete the sentences by providing the correct words for the family relationships in the blanks.

Example: **Christas Mann heißt Werner.**

1. **Christas** [   ] **heißt Dagmar und ihre** [   ]

    heißen Matthias und Thomas.

2. **Matthias hat zwei** [   ] **: eine** [   ] **und**

    einen [   ] **.**

3. **Dagmar ist verheiratet: Ihr** [   ] **heißt Erich.**

4. **Dagmar und Erich haben zwei** [   ] **: Olivia und Mark.**

5. **Dagmar ist Marks** [   ] **und Erich ist sein**

    [   ] **.**

6. **Christa ist Olivias** [   ] **und Werner ist Olivias**

    [   ] **.**

7. **Erichs** [   ] **heißt Dagmar.**

8. **Werners** [   ] **heißen Olivia und Mark.**

6. Write sentences stating what jobs these people do.

Example: **Gabi Franke:** photographer   **Gabi Franke ist Fotografin.**

a. **Dieter Hanschke:** construction worker

b. **Jürgen Schumacher:** hair stylist

c. **Birgit Harms:** teacher

d. **Uwe Balzer:** nurse

e. **Renate Bachmann:** cashier

7. Find the 10 greeting and goodbye expressions. They all run in a straight line—vertically, horizontally or diagonally.

A	U	F	E	D	R	S	E	H	E	H	O	Ü	H
U	U	Ü	R	**G**	**U**	**T**	**E**	**N**	**T**	**A**	**G**	G	I
F	Ö	F	G	A	T	Ö	R	E	H	L	T	H	T
R	G	A	W	U	T	S	T	L	N	L	S	A	T
E	D	U	J	I	T	E	C	S	S	O	E	K	C
U	D	U	T	M	E	E	A	H	C	H	R	C	H
T	W	A	T	E	T	D	N	A	Ü	E	V	I	Ü
M	T	I	S	E	N	G	E	A	U	S	U	A	N
I	A	S	E	I	N	M	N	R	C	A	S	O	H
C	D	T	C	Y	S	M	O	S	H	H	B	Ü	H
H	D	H	F	W	E	T	O	R	R	Ö	T	S	T
F	T	E	N	A	B	E	D	R	G	Ö	R	H	G
A	U	F	W	I	E	D	E	R	S	E	H	E	N
U	F	W	I	E	D	E	H	Ü	S	S	N	E	N

Lesson 10 — A Double Room with a Shower, Please.

Ein Doppelzimmer mit Dusche, bitte.

LESSON OBJECTIVES

Lesson 10 is about booking a hotel room. When you have completed this lesson, you'll know how to:

- ask about facilities
- check into a hotel

DIALOGUE

 Listen to these people at the reception desk in the Hotel Grunewald in Berlin.

Empfangschef:	**Guten Tag. Was wünschen Sie?**
	Good afternoon. Can I help you?
Herr Bachmann:	**Guten Tag. Ich habe ein Zimmer bestellt.**
	Good afternoon. I've reserved a room.
Empfangschef:	**Wie ist Ihr Name, bitte?**
	What's your name, please?
Herr Bachmann:	**Bachmann.**
	Bachmann.
Empfangschef:	**Ach ja, Herr Bachmann. Zimmer 123. Füllen Sie bitte das Formular aus. Danke.**
	Oh yes, Mr. Bachmann. Room 123. Please fill out this form. Thank you.

. . . .

Empfangschef:	**Guten Tag. Was wünschen Sie?**
	Good afternoon. Can I help you?
Frau Armbruster:	**Guten Tag. Ich habe ein Zimmer bestellt. Mein Name ist Armbruster.**
	Good afternoon. I've reserved a room. My name is Armbruster.
Empfangschef:	**Frau Armbruster ... Moment ... Ja, Zimmer 117. Füllen Sie bitte das Formular aus. Danke.**
	Frau Armbruster...just a moment...Yes, room 117. Please fill out this form. Thank you.

1. **DIALOGUE ACTIVITY**

What is each person's room number?

Use the following words and expressions to
guide you through the lesson.

ab + reisen	to leave, depart
alles	all, everything
Alles belegt.	All taken./ No vacancy.
das Anmeldeformular (-e)	registration form
die Anschrift (-en)	address
aus + füllen	to fill out
die Ausweisnummer (-n)	ID number, passport number
das Bad (¨-er)	bath
belegt	occupied, taken
bestellen	to order
bleiben	to stay
Das ist zu teuer!	That's too expensive!
das Doppelzimmer (-)	double room
die Dusche (-n)	shower
das Einzelzimmer (-)	single room
extra	extra
das Formular (-e)	form
frei	free, vacant
das Frühstück	breakfast
Füllen Sie bitte das Formular aus.	Fill out the form, please.
Haben Sie ein Doppelzimmer frei?	Do you have a double room free?

heute	today
Ich habe ein Zimmer reserviert.	I've reserved a room.
Ich nehme es für eine Nacht.	I'll take it for one night.
Ich reise heute ab.	I'm leaving today.
inklusive	included, inclusive
Ist das ein Zimmer mit Bad?	Is that a room with a bath?
der Moment (-e)	moment
die Nacht (¨-e)	night
nehmen	to take
oje	oh dear
die Person (-en)	person
pro	per
reservieren	to reserve
teuer	expensive
das WC (-s)	toilet, WC
wenigstens	at least
Wie lange?	How long?
willkommen	welcome
Wir sind ein Hotel garni.	This is a "hotel garni." (a hotel that provides bed and breakfast)
die Woche (-n)	week
das Zimmer (-)	room

2. LISTENING ACTIVITY

 Now listen to some more people at the reception desk in the Hotel Grunewald in Berlin and fill in their room numbers.

Empfangschef:	**Guten Tag. Kann ich etwas für Sie tun?**
	Good afternoon. Can I help you?
Herr Bader:	**Ich reise heute ab. Mein Name ist Bader,**
	Zimmer [ ]**.**
	I'm leaving today. My name is Bader, room…
Empfangschef:	**Hier ist Ihre Rechnung, Herr Bader.**
	Here's your bill, Mr. Bader.

Empfangschef:	**Guten Tag. Kann ich etwas für Sie tun?**
	Good afternoon. Can I help you?
Frau Reisner:	**Guten Tag. Reisner ist mein Name. Ich habe ein Zimmer**
	bestellt.
	Hello. My name is Reisner. I have reserved a room.
Empfangschef:	**Frau Reisner … Zimmer** [ ]**. Füllen Sie bitte**
	das Formular aus. Danke.
	Mrs. Reisner…room… Fill out the form, please. Thank you.

DID YOU KNOW?

 There are tourist offices in every German town that will give you information about where to stay, where to eat and what to do, and they usually provide free maps of the city. Moreover, the tourist offices frequently have beautifully produced posters and booklets of their towns or regions which you can obtain free either at the office or by mail.

3. WRITING ACTIVITY

Can you write out the numbers in words? The first two have been done for you, and the pattern is completely regular, but remember to put the units before the tens.

101   (ein)hunderteins

121   hunderteinundzwanzig

201

221

199

257

375

999

Ruhrlandmuseum
Route der Industriekultur

Margarethenhöhe →
Route der Industriekultur

DID YOU KNOW?

Most German towns have handy signs posted to direct you to the most important places in the town.

4. LISTENING ACTIVITY

Listen to these guests ask about available rooms, then complete the details of the three hotels.

	Hotel 1	Hotel 2	Hotel 3
Einzelzimmer pro Nacht	80,–	_____,–	_____,–
Doppelzimmer pro Nacht	_____,–	75,–	_____,–
mit WC	_____	ja	
mit Dusche/Bad	_____	_____	
mit Frühstück	_____	_____	nein

1

Frau: **Was kostet ein Doppelzimmer pro Nacht?**

Empfangschef: **110€.**

Frau: **Und ein Einzelzimmer?**

Empfangschef: **80€.**

Frau: **Ist Frühstück inklusive?**

Empfangschef: **Ja.**

Frau: **Ist das Zimmer mit Bad?**

Empfangschef: **Ja, alle Zimmer haben Bad, Dusche und WC.**

Frau: **Gut, danke. Wiederhören.**

2

Empfangschefin: **Guten Abend. Sie wünschen?**

Mann: **Guten Abend. Was kostet hier ein Einzelzimmer pro Nacht?**

Empfangschefin:	60€ Euro pro Nacht. Aber alle Einzelzimmer sind belegt.
Mann:	Oje! Haben Sie ein Doppelzimmer frei?
Empfangschefin:	Ja, ein Doppelzimmer mit Dusche kostet dann 75€ pro Nacht.
Mann:	Ach so ... Ist Frühstück inklusive?
Empfangschefin:	Ja, wir sind ein Hotel garni.
Mann:	Ja, gut. Ich nehme es für eine Nacht.

3

Empfangschef:	Guten Abend. Wie kann ich Ihnen helfen?
Frau:	Haben Sie zwei Einzelzimmer frei?
Empfangschef:	Ja, für 90€ pro Zimmer pro Nacht.
Frau:	Das ist teuer! Und ein Doppelzimmer?
Empfangschef:	120€ pro Nacht.
Frau:	Oje! Das ist auch sehr teuer. Ist Frühstück wenigstens inklusive?
Empfangschef:	Nein, Frühstück ist 12€ extra pro Person.

Separable Verbs: *abreisen, ausfüllen*

GRAMMAR

Did you notice that "I'm leaving" is *ich reise ab*, but the infinitive "to leave" is *abreisen*? Similarly "I fill out (a form)" is *ich fülle (ein Formular) aus*, but the infinitive "to fill out" is *ausfüllen*. These are separable verbs: they consist of a normal verb and a preposition. In the infinitive form, the preposition is prefixed to the verb, but when the verb is used with a subject, the preposition goes to the end of the sentence:

| *aus + füllen* | *Ich fülle es aus.* | I fill it out. |
| *ab + reisen* | *Ich reise heute ab.* | I leave today. |

All separable verbs are marked by + between the prefix and verb in the Vocabulary section.

105

5. SPEAKING ACTIVITY 66 99

 You'd like a double room at the Hotel Spreewald. Practice what you're going to say first, then play the audio file to check your answers.

Empfangschefin: **Guten Abend! Kann ich etwas für Sie tun?**

Sie: Ask if she has a double room available.

Empfangschefin: **Wie lange möchten Sie bleiben?**

Sie: Three nights.

Empfangschefin: **Ja, wir haben ein Doppelzimmer frei. Das kostet neunzig Euro pro Nacht.**

Sie: Ask if breakfast is included.

Empfangschefin: **Ja, Frühstück ist inklusive.**

Sie: Say you'll take it.

6. WRITING ACTIVITY

Fill out this hotel registration form.

Hotel Spreewald
Anmeldeformular

Familienname:

Vorname:

ANSCHRIFT

Straße/Nummer:

PLZ/Wohnort:

Land:

Ausweisnummer:

7. SPEAKING ACTIVITY

Pretend you are looking for a hotel room. Follow the prompts in the dialogues below.

1

Sie: Ask the price of a double room per night.

Empfangschef: 210 €.

Sie: Ask how much a single room is.

Empfangschef: 150 €.

Sie: Ask if breakfast is included.

Empfangschef: Ja.

Sie: Ask if the room has a bath.

Empfangschef: Ja, alle Zimmer haben Bad, Dusche und WC.

Sie: Say thank you and goodbye.

- -

2   **Empfangschef: Guten Abend. Wie kann ich Ihnen helfen?**

Sie: Ask if there are two single rooms available.

Empfangschef: Ja, für 100 € pro Zimmer pro Nacht.

Sie: Say that you think it's too expensive and ask about the possibility of a double room.

Empfangschef: 120 € pro Nacht.

Sie: Exclaim that you think it is also expensive. Ask if breakfast is included in the price.

Empfangschef: Ja, ja.

8. SPEAKING ACTIVITY

Can you say the following phrases in German?

1. **Room number 474.**

2. **I have reserved a room.**

3. **I'm leaving today.**

4. **I'd like a double room with a shower.**

5. **Do you have any rooms free?**

Check It!

Test what you've learned in this lesson and review anything you're not sure of.

CAN YOU . . . ?

say you've reserved a room
Ich habe ein Zimmer bestellt/
reserviert.

count from 101–999
hunderteins, hundertzwei, … ,
neunhundertneunundneunzig

**specify what kind of room
you want**
Ich möchte ein Einzelzimmer/
Doppelzimmer mit Bad/Dusche.

**ask whether breakfast
is included**
Ist Frühstück inklusive?

BERLITZ   HOTSPOT   Go to www.berlitzhotspot.com for…

Social Networking
Do you have any hotel recommendations in German-speaking countries? Go to the **Berlitz Hotspot** and share them with your friends.

Podcast 10
Where to Sleep?
Download the podcast

Internet Activity
Are you interested in more practice concerning hotels? Go to **Berlitz Hotspot** to access links to hotel websites. Practice making requests based on what you've learned in this lesson.

Video 6 – **Hotel Check-in**
A woman checks in at a German hotel. What is her room number? What are the directions to her room? Watch the video and learn how to check in at a hotel and listen to directions.

Lesson 11 | Where Is The...?

Wo ist hier ... ?

LESSON OBJECTIVES

Lesson 11 is about asking for directions. When you have completed this lesson, you'll know how to:

- ask for directions
- refer to different places of business

DIALOGUE

 Listen to some people asking for directions to certain places around town.

1

Mann 1: **Entschuldigung, wo ist hier eine Post?**
Excuse me, where is the post office around here?

Mann 2: **Gleich um die Ecke.**
Just around the corner.

2

Frau: **Entschuldigung, wo ist hier ein Restaurant?**
Excuse me, where is a restaurant around here?

Mann: **Da vorne rechts, sehen Sie?**
Over there on the right, can you see it?

3

Mann: **Entschuldigung, wo ist hier ein Café?**
Excuse me, where is a café around here?

Frau: **Da vorne links.**
Over there on the left.

1. DIALOGUE ACTIVITY

Which places do the people want to go?

Use the following words and expressions to guide you through the lesson.

VOCABULARY

an (+ dat.)	at	leicht	easy
auf der rechten Seite	on the right	links	left
		der Meter (-)	meter
(Das ist) ganz leicht zu finden.	That's very easy to find.	neben (+ dat.)	next to
		noch mal	again
die Bäckerei (-en)	bakery	die Post	post office
die Bank (-en)	bank	rechts	right
der Blumenladen (-läden)	flower shop, florist's	sehen	to see
die Buchhandlung (-en)	bookstore	die Seite (-n)	side
		die Straße (-n)	street, road
das Café (-s)	café	der Taxistand (¨-e)	taxi stand
da vorne	over there	die Telefonzelle (-n)	phone booth
(Das) weiß ich auch nicht.	I don't know that either.	die U-Bahn-Station (-en)	subway station
die Ecke (-n)	corner	um (+ acc.)	around
Entschuldigung!	Excuse me!	verstehen	to understand
(es) tut mir leid	I'm sorry	vielleicht	perhaps
finden	to find	Vielleicht vierhundert Meter weiter.	Maybe 400 meters farther on.
der Geldautomat (-en)	ATM, cash machine		
		vor (+ dat.)	in front of
gehen	to go	war	was (infinitive: sein)
geradeaus	straight ahead		
gleich	just, immediately	weiß	know (infinitive: wissen)
das Hotel (-s)	hotel		
Ich bin nicht von hier.	I'm not from around here.	weiter	further
		Wie bitte?	Pardon?
(Ich) weiß (es) nicht.	I don't know.	Wo?	Where?
immer	always	der Zeitungshändler (-)	newsstand
die Kreuzung (-en)	intersection, junction		
der Laden (¨)	shop, store	zum (= zu dem)	to the (masculine and neuter)
langsamer	slower, more slowly		

2. **ACTIVITY**

You want the following items; where would you find them? Match the items to the places in the box. (Some items can be found in more than one place.)

1	die Post	4	das Restaurant	7	die Buchhandlung
2	der Zeitungshändler	5	die Bank	8	der Geldautomat
3	das Café	6	der Blumenladen		

a. ☐   b. ☐   c. ☐

d. ☐   e. ☐   f. ☐

3. **WRITING ACTIVITY**

Insert *eine* or *ein* in the blank as appropriate:

a. **Entschuldigung, wo ist hier** ☐ **Post?**

b. **Entschuldigung, wo ist hier** ☐ **Restaurant?**

c. **Entschuldigung, wo ist hier** ☐ **Café?**

d. **Entschuldigung, wo ist hier** ☐ **Buchhandlung?**

e. **Entschuldigung, wo ist hier** ☐ **Blumenladen?**

f. **Entschuldigung, wo ist hier** ☐ **Zeitungshändler?**

g. **Entschuldigung, wo ist hier** ☐ **Bank?**

h. **Entschuldigung, wo ist hier** ☐ **Geldautomat?**

4. LISTENING ACTIVITY

 Choose the correct diagram to illustrate each dialogue. (Some diagrams match more than one dialogue.)

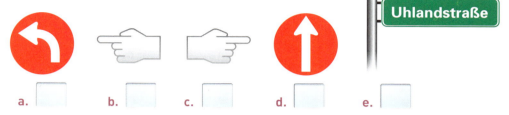

a. ☐   b. ☐   c. ☐   d. ☐   e. ☐

1

Mann 1: **Entschuldigung, wo ist hier eine Post?**

Mann 2: **Gleich um die Ecke.**

2

Frau: **Entschuldigung, wo ist hier ein Restaurant?**

Mann: **Da vorne rechts, sehen Sie?**

3

Mann: **Entschuldigung, wo ist hier ein Café?**

Frau: **Da vorne links.**

4

Mann: **Entschuldigung, wo ist hier eine Buchhandlung?**

Frau: **Gehen Sie gradeaus.**

5

Mann: **Entschuldigung, wo ist hier ein Blumenladen?**

Frau: **Immer geradeaus.**

6

Frau: **Entschuldigung, wo ist hier ein Zeitungshändler?**

Mann: **In der Uhlandstraße.**

7

Frau 1: **Entschuldigung, wo ist hier eine Bank?**

Frau 2: **Um die Ecke.**

8

Mann 1: **Entschuldigung, wo ist hier ein Geldautomat?**

Mann 2: **Da vorne rechts.**

5. LISTENING ACTIVITY

Listen to the directions. Match these places with the letters on the map. You can refer to expressions on the next page for help if you like.

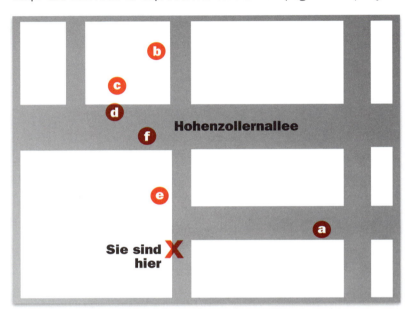

1. [   ]   **Hotel Spreewald**   4. [   ]   **Bäckerei**

2. [   ]   **Café Dreiklang**   5. [   ]   **Taxistand**

3. [   ]   **U-Bahn-Station Uhlandstraße**   6. [   ]   **Telefonzelle**

| Mann 1: | Entschuldigung, wie komme ich zum Hotel Spreewald? |
| Mann 2: | Tja ... gehen Sie gradeaus bis zur nächsten Querstraße. Dann links in die Hohenzollernallee. Das Hotel ist auf der rechten Seite. |

| Mann: | Entschuldigung, wie komme ich zum Café Dreiklang? |
| Frau: | Gehen Sie immer gradeaus, vielleicht 400 Meter weiter. Das Café ist auf der linken Seite. |

Mann 1:   **Entschuldigung, wo ist die U-Bahn-Station Uhlandstraße?**

Frau: **Tut mir leid, das weiß ich auch nicht. Ich bin nicht von hier.**

Mann 2:   **Ach ja, das ist hier rechts um die Ecke; ganz leicht zu finden.**

Mann: **Entschuldigung, wo ist hier eine Bäckerei?**

Frau: **Da vorne links. Sehen Sie?**

Mann 1:   **Entschuldigung, wo ist hier ein Taxistand?**

Frau: **Weiß ich nicht.**

Mann 2:   **In der Hohenzollernallee, vor dem Hotel Spreewald.**

Mann: **Entschuldigung, wo ist hier eine Telefonzelle?**

Frau: **Gehen Sie gradeaus und dann um die Ecke links.**

6. LISTENING ACTIVITY

Listen now to some questions you can ask if you did not understand; each is repeated. Fill in the missing word.

a.   _____ **bitte?**

b.   **Wie war das noch** _____ **?**

c.   _____ **, bitte!**

d.   **Wie** _____ **die Straße?**

e.   _____ **Sie das buchstabieren?**

f.   **Ich verstehe** _____ **.**

7. LISTENING ACTIVITY

 Listen to the tour of the Tiergarten Park in Berlin. Can you put names to the sights? One of the sights doesn't belong on the map. Which one is it?

Brandenburger Tor

Gedächtnis- kirche

Siegessäule

Fernsehturm

Kongresshalle

Hier ist die Siegessäule.

Rechts, etwa 300 Meter weiter, ist das Brandenburger Tor.

Oder gehen Sie rechts immer gradeaus bis zur nächsten Querstraße, dann links: Die Kongresshalle ist auf der linken Seite.

Oder gehen Sie durch den Tiergarten immer geradeaus: Dort ist die Gedächtniskirche.

Links von der Gedächtniskirche, immer geradeaus, vielleicht 200 Meter weiter, ist der Fernsehturm.

Instructions and Commands

GRAMMAR

When instructing someone to do something, you can use the imperative or command form. The verb comes at the beginning of the sentence, just like in a question:

Sie gehen geradeaus.	You go straight ahead. (statement)
Gehen Sie geradeaus?	Are you going straight ahead? (question)
Gehen Sie geradeaus!	Go straight ahead! (instruction)

If you address someone formally, in German you literally say "Go you straight ahead", not just "Go straight ahead", like English.

8. **WRITING ACTIVITY**

A German friend of yours is coming for a visit. He wants to know where he can find the closest *Restaurant*, *Geldautomat* and *Post* in your town. Write him an email giving him this information.

An: freund@de.com

Von:

Betreff: Hallo!

SENDEN   LÖSCHEN

Compound Nouns and Gender

GRAMMAR

As you'll have noticed, German has some very long words! However, these are usually just two or more words written together (compounds). If you can recognize the components, grasping the meaning of the compound isn't usually a problem. For example:

die Blumen + der Laden = der Blumenladen

the flowers + the shop = the flower shop (literally: the flowers shop)

Compound nouns like *Blumenladen* take the gender of the last component: it's *die Blume* but *der Laden*, so it's *der Blumenladen*.

9. WRITING ACTIVITY

Separate the components of the following compound words.

1. **der Blumenladen**

2. **die Buchhandlung**

3. **der Geldautomat**

4. **der Taxistand**

5. **die U-Bahn-Station**

6. **der Zeitungshändler**

Check It!

Test what you've learned in this lesson and review anything you're not sure of.

CAN YOU . . . ?

☐ **ask your way to various stores and services**
Wo ist hier eine Post/ein Café/ eine Buchhandlung?

☐ **say you don't understand**
Ich verstehe nicht.

☐ **say "Pardon?"**
Wie bitte?

☐ **ask someone to speak more slowly**
Langsamer, bitte!

☐ **ask someone to repeat**
Wie war das noch mal?

BERLITZ   HOTSPOT   Go to www.berlitzhotspot.com for...

 Social Networking
Go to **Berlitz Hotspot** and share your local culture with your Hotspot friends. What's the most important site to visit in your town? Be sure to tell your friends the relevant information, so they can visit some day!

 Podcast 11
Munich
Download the podcast.

 Internet Activity
Are you interested in learning more about large German-speaking cities? Use your favorite search engine to access a German, Austrian or Swiss city you'd like to visit and see if you can locate a tourist map. Select a handful of attractions and see if you can come up with mini-dialogues of people asking for/giving directions to each.

Wie viel Uhr ist es?

LESSON OBJECTIVES

Lesson 12 is about opening and closing times. When you have completed this lesson, you'll know how to:

- state the time and the day
- ask about and give opening times

DIALOGUE

Listen to these newscasters announcing the time.

Guten Morgen, liebe Hörerinnen und Hörer. Willkommen zu den Nachrichten um sechs Uhr dreißig.

Guten Morgen, liebe Hörerinnen und Hörer. Hier sind die Nachrichten um acht Uhr.

1. DIALOGUE ACTIVITY

What times are mentioned in the dialogues?

Use the following words and expressions to guide you through the lesson.

die Bibliothek (-en)	library	**der Ruhetag (-e)**	day off, closed day
bis	to, until	**(die) Uhr (-en)**	clock, o'clock (in times)
die Dame (-n)	lady		
der Gast (¨-e)	guest	**um**	at
geöffnet	open, opened	**um ... Uhr**	at...o'clock
geschlossen	closed	**Um wie viel Uhr?**	At what time?
halb zwei	half past one (lit.: half to two)	**Viertel nach/vor**	a quarter after/to
		von	from
der Herr (-en)	gentleman, man	**vor**	to, before
lieb	dear	**Wann?**	When?
nach	past, after	**Wie spät ist es?**	How late is it?
die Nachrichten (pl.)	news	**Wie viel?**	How much?
die Öffnungszeiten (pl.)	opening times		

DID YOU KNOW?

By law, German stores and shops—big and small, urban and rural—are allowed to remain open 80 hours per week within the following framework:

· Legal business hours in Germany are usually 9 a.m. to 8 p.m. Monday through Saturday.

· On Sundays, bakeries only are permitted to open. Business hours are usually from 7 a.m. to 11 a.m.

In Switzerland stores usually close around 6.30 p.m.; in bigger cities they close at 8 p.m. (Monday to Friday). On Saturdays shops are open to 4 p.m. or 5 p.m. On Sundays all businesses are closed.

In Austria, stores open around 8 a.m. Many, however, close for a two-hour lunch break. On Sundays, all businesses are closed, with the exception of bakeries.

2. **LISTENING ACTIVITY**

Wie viel Uhr ist es? What time is it? Listen to the audio file first, then complete the times below. Note that each time is repeated.

A. **Es ist** _____ **Uhr.**

B. **Es ist** _____ **Uhr.**

C. **Es ist** _____ **Uhr.**

D. **Es ist** _____ **Uhr.**

E. _____ **Uhr dreißig.**

F. **halb** _____

G. _____ **Uhr dreißig.**

H. **halb** _____

3. LISTENING ACTIVITY

At what times do these news bulletins occur? Use the 24-hour clock in your answers.

1. [   ]   2. [   ]   3. [   ]   4. [   ]

Nachrichtensprecher 1: Guten Tag, meine Damen und Herren. Hier sind die Nachrichten um dreizehn Uhr dreißig.

Nachrichtensprecherin 1: Fünfzehn Uhr. Guten Tag, meine Damen und Herren. Sie hören Nachrichten.

Nachrichtensprecher 2: Guten Abend, liebe Hörerinnen und Hörer. Hier sind die Nachrichten um neunzehn Uhr dreißig.

Nachrichtensprecherin 2: Es ist zweiundzwanzig Uhr. Sie hören Nachrichten.

4. LISTENING ACTIVITY

Below are the German words for Monday to Sunday, but with the letters scrambled. Can you rearrange them? Remember to begin each one with a capital letter.

a. **gamnot**   [   ]

b. **adeginst**   [   ]

c. **chimottw**   [   ]

d. **degnanorst**   [   ]

e. **efgirat**   [   ]

f. **gamsast**   [   ]

g. **gannost**   [   ]

5. LISTENING ACTIVITY

 Match the signs with the recorded messages.

1

Wir haben montags bis mittwochs zehn Uhr bis neunzehn Uhr dreißig geöffnet; donnerstags von zehn bis einundzwanzig Uhr; freitags von zehn bis neunzehn Uhr dreißig und samstags von zehn bis dreizehn Uhr. Sonntag ist Ruhetag.

2

Wir haben montags geschlossen. Wir haben dienstags bis samstags von zehn bis siebzehn Uhr geöffnet und sonntags von elf bis siebzehn Uhr.

3

Wir haben montags bis freitags von acht bis neunzehn Uhr geöffnet, sonnabends von acht bis sechzehn Uhr und sonntags von zehn bis sechzehn Uhr.

Days of the Week

To say that something happens regularly "on Mondays", "on Tuesdays", etc., add -s to the day of the week:

Die Bibliothek hat montags von neun bis neunzehn Uhr geöffnet; dienstags …
The library is open on Mondays from nine A.M. to seven P.M.; on Tuesdays…

You write *montags, dienstags*, etc., with a lower case letter, but you write *Montag, Dienstag*, etc. with a capital.

6. **WRITING ACTIVITY**

Write a short text like those you heard in Activity 5 to communicate the opening hours for *Zu Tisch Restaurant*.

Zu Tisch Restaurant

MO GESCHLOSSEN:
Di – Do 12-15 Uhr/17-22 Uhr
Fr – Sa 12-15 Uhr/17-24 Uhr
So 12-15 Uhr

127

7. SPEAKING ACTIVITY

You're working in your local tourist office, and a German tourist phones to ask what times you're open. Here are the times. How are you going to state them in German? Write down your answers, then say them aloud.

Monday–Friday: 9–16:00

Saturday: 9–18:00

Sunday: closed

Tourist: **Wann haben Sie montags bis freitags geöffnet?**

Sie: **Wir haben montags** ⬚ **geöffnet.**

Tourist: **Und samstags?**

Sie: **Wir haben samstags** ⬚ **geöffnet.**

Tourist: **Und sonntags?**

Sie: **Sonntags haben wir** ⬚ .

8. LISTENING ACTIVITY

Rabea's keeping a note of what she's doing and when. Match the events with the days Rabea plans to participate in them.

a. **Mittwoch, 12:45 Uhr**   A. **ein Konzert in der Philharmonie**

b. **Dienstag, 12 Uhr**   B. **eine Havelrundfahrt**

c. **Montag, 11 Uhr**   C. **eine Führung durch das Neue Palais**

d. **Sonntag, 10 Uhr**   D. **ein Besuch der Filmstudios**

e. **Samstag, 20 Uhr**   E. **eine Stadtrundfahrt durch Potsdam**

Rabea: **Also, ich habe fünf Tage in Potsdam und möchte viel sehen. Am Samstagabend um zwanzig Uhr gibt es ein Konzert in der Philharmonie, Strawinsky. Das ist herrlich! Am Sonntag um zehn Uhr mache ich eine Bootsfahrt auf der Havel. Hoffentlich ist es schön! Am Montag um elf Uhr besuche ich die Filmstudios. Ich bin großer Filmfan und finde das total interessant. Am Dienstag um zwölf Uhr mittags gibt es eine Führung durch das Neue Palais, und am Mittwoch um zwölf Uhr fünfundvierzig mache ich eine Stadtrundfahrt durch Potsdam.**

Word Order

In German, you can change the word order for emphasis, but the verb must come second in the sentence.

For example:

Montags hat die Bibliothek von neun bis neunzehn Uhr geöffnet.

On Mondays, the library is open from nine a.m. to seven p.m.

PRONUNCIATION

 How would you pronounce these words? Now, listen to the audio file to practice your pronunciation.

leicht

weiter

Seite

Wien

wieder

sieben

Check It! Test what you've learned in this lesson and review anything you're not sure of.

CAN YOU . . . ?

☐ state the time
Es ist ein Uhr.
Es ist halb drei.
Es ist Viertel vor sieben.

☐ state opening times
Wir haben montags von acht Uhr bis siebzehn Uhr geöffnet.

☐ list the days of the week
Montag, Dienstag, Mittwoch, Donnerstag, Freitag, Samstag (Sonnabend), Sonntag

Learn More

Collect German-language brochures for tourist attractions. They often give hours of operation, written instructions and maps showing how to get there. See how much of the information you understand.

 Go to www.berlitzhotspot.com for...

BERLITZ HOTSPOT

Social Networking
Go to **Berlitz Hotspot** and tell your friends about your schedule. Do you work or study the typical 9-5, Monday through Friday, or do you have a more varied schedule?

Podcast 12
Business Hours
Download the podcast

Internet Activity
Are you interested in more practice with schedules? Look for some German-speaking businesses online and practice giving their opening hours aloud.

Wo kann ich Postkarten kaufen?

Lesson 13 is about buying items. When you have completed this lesson, you'll know how to:

- ask where you can buy items
- talk about different kinds of shops

DIALOGUE

 We asked passers-by in Berlin where we could buy several items.

1

Frau 1: **Entschuldigung, wo kann ich hier einen Kugelschreiber kaufen?**
Excuse me, where can I buy a ballpoint pen around here?

Frau 2: **Im Schreibwarenladen. An der nächsten Ecke links.**
At the stationery store. At the next corner on the left.

2

Frau 1: **Entschuldigung, wo kann ich hier eine Zeitung kaufen?**
Excuse me, where can I buy a newspaper around here?

Frau 2: **Äh, am Zeitungskiosk. Geradeaus und dann rechts.**
At the newspaper kiosk. Straight ahead and then on the right.

3

Frau: **Entschuldigung, wo kann ich hier Kopfschmerztabletten kaufen?**
Excuse me, where can I buy aspirin around here?

Mann: **Die nächste Apotheke ist 100 Meter weiter. Auf der rechten Seite.**
The next pharmacy is 100 meters down the street. On the right.

1. DIALOGUE ACTIVITY

What were the items?

Use the following words and expressions to guide you through the lesson.

VOCABULARY

die Apotheke (-n)	pharmacy
die Briefmarke (-n)	(postage) stamp
der Computer (-)	computer
die Dachterrasse (-n)	roof terrace
die Damenmode (-n)	ladies' fashion
die Damenwäsche	lingerie
dort	there
dritte	third
der Einkaufsbummel (-)	shopping spree
das Elektrogerät (-e)	electrical appliance
das Erdgeschoss	first floor (US), ground floor (UK)
erste	first
die Etage (-n)	floor, story
der Etagenplan (-pläne)	floor plan, store plan (in department store, etc.)
gegenüber von (+ dat.)	opposite
die Haushaltswaren (pl.)	household items
die Herrenmode (-n)	men's fashion
die Herrenwäsche	men's underwear
kaufen	to buy
können (ich kann, er kann)	to be able
die Kopfschmerztablette (-n)	aspirin (lit. headache tablet)
die Kosmetika (pl.)	cosmetics
der Kugelschreiber (-)	ballpoint pen
die Lebensmittel (pl.)	food, groceries
nächste	next
das Obst	fruit
der Obsthändler (-)	fruit seller
die Parfümerie (-n)	perfumery
der/die Passant/-in	(male/female) passer-by
das Porzellan	porcelain, china
der Schreibwarenladen (-läden)	stationery store
die Spielwaren (pl.)	toys
die Sportartikel (pl.)	sports goods
trinken	to drink
vierte	fourth
die Zeitung (-en)	newspaper
zweite	second

Word Order

GRAMMAR

Remember: When there are two verbs in a sentence, the second verb comes at the end:

Wo kann ich hier eine Zeitung kaufen?
Where can I buy a newspaper here?

2. **WRITING ACTIVITY**

How would you ask where to buy each of these items?

a. a newspaper

b. a ballpoint pen

c. medication

d. fruit

e. stamps

f. bread

134

3. LISTENING ACTIVITY

 When prompted, ask where you can buy each of the items from Activity 2. Listen to the directions you are given, and complete the key to the map.

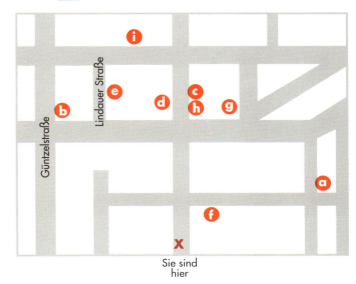

Sie sind
hier

Schlüssel

a =
b =
c =
d =
e =
f =
g = Café
h = Bank
i = Supermarkt

Sie: Ask where you can buy a newspaper here.

Mann: **Gehen Sie immer gradeaus. Zwei Straßen weiter ist eine Bank. Neben der Bank ist ein Zeitungshändler.**

Sie: Ask where you can buy a ballpoint pen.

Frau: **Tja ... in der Lindauer Straße ist ein Schreibwarenladen. Nehmen Sie die zweite Straße links, und die erste Straße rechts ist dann die Lindauer Straße.**

Sie: Ask where you can buy aspirin.

Frau: **Gehen Sie immer geradeaus. Zwei Straßen weiter sehen Sie eine Bank. Gegenüber von der Bank ist eine Apotheke.**

Sie: Ask where you can buy fruit.

Mann: **Nehmen Sie die nächste Straße rechts, dann die erste links. Dort ist ein Obsthändler.**

Sie: Ask where you can buy stamps.

Frau: **Gleich um die Ecke rechts ist eine Post.**

Sie: Ask where you can buy bread.

Frau: **Brot? In der Güntzelstraße ist eine Bäckerei. Nehmen Sie die zweite Straße links, dann die zweite rechts. Die Bäckerei ist gleich an der Ecke.**

GRAMMAR

To create ordinal numbers, the basic pattern is to add *-te* to the cardinal number (one, two, etc.), but there are some irregular forms:

first	*erste*	sixth	*sechste*
second	*zweite*	seventh	*siebte*
third	*dritte*	eighth	*achte*
fourth	*vierte*	ninth	*neunte*
fifth	*fünfte*	tenth	*zehnte*

When written as a figure, ordinals have a period after the number. So *(die) erste Etage* would be written *1. Etage,* and so on.

4. LISTENING ACTIVITY

Listen to the dialogues once again. Did you notice the ordinals when they said "the first street", "the second street" and so on? Write down the examples that you hear for each dialogue.

1.

2.

3.

4.

5.

6.

5. **SPEAKING ACTIVITY**

Some people ask you the following questions. Give them directions in German to the appropriate places on the map.

a. Passant: **Entschuldigung! Wo kann ich hier einen Kaffee trinken?**

Sie: **Gehen Sie** _____.

b. Passantin: **Entschuldigen Sie, wo kann ich hier Lebensmittel kaufen?**

Sie: _____.

c. Passantin: **Entschuldigen Sie, wo kann ich hier Brötchen kaufen?**

Sie: _____.

6. **LISTENING ACTIVITY**

 Here's some more practice with ordinals. Listen to the audio file and then fill in the floor numbers in the picture.

Sechste Etage.
Dachterrassencafé.

Erste Etage.
Damenmode und Damenwäsche.

Fünfte Etage.
Elektrogeräte und Computer.

Dritte Etage.
Haushaltswaren und Porzellan.

Zweite Etage.
Herrenmode und Herrenwäsche.

Erdgeschoss.
Kosmetika und Parfümerie.

Vierte Etage.
Spielwaren und Sportartikel.

7. WRITING ACTIVITY

Now create the *Etagenplan* for your own store. Write out the floor numbers using ordinals and then list what items are available on that floor. Try using an English-German dictionary to list individual items. Follow the example below.

Erdgeschoss: Apotheke (Ibuprofen, Kopfschmerztablette, Pflaster)

8. **WRITING ACTIVITY**

Here's a look at the businesses on *Mozartstraße*. Using the vocabulary that you have learned in this lesson, make statements or questions about the businesses.

Example: **Kann ich Kopfschmerztabletten in der Apotheke kaufen?**

Check It!

Test what you've learned in this lesson and review anything you're not sure of.

CAN YOU . . . ?

☐ **ask where you can buy commonly needed items**
Wo kann ich hier einen Kugelschreiber/eine Zeitung/Brot/Obst kaufen?

☐ **give directions to a place**
Gehen Sie geradeaus.
Nehmen Sie die erste/zweite/dritte Straße links/rechts.

☐ **describe locations**
Neben der Bank.
Gegenüber von der Bank.
In der Lindauer Straße.

☐ **give floor numbers**
Erdgeschoss, erste/zweite/dritte/vierte/fünfte/sechste Etage

BERLITZ HOTSPOT   Go to www.berlitzhotspot.com for...

Social Networking
Have you ever been shopping in Europe? Go to **Berlitz Hotspot** and share your stories with your Hotspot friends.

Internet Activity
Visit the online sites of chocolatiers in Germany, Austria and Switzerland. Make a list of the different kinds of chocolate offered, then practice asking for these chocolates out loud. For more practice, find the shop locations on the websites, then give directions to the chocolate shops in German.

Podcast 13
Der Zeitungskiosk
Download the podcas[t]

Ich suche ein gestreiftes Hemd.

LESSON OBJECTIVES

Lesson 14 is about buying clothes. When you have completed this lesson, you'll know how to:

- talk about clothing
- request colors and patterns

DIALOGUE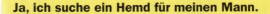

Listen as Julia shops for clothes.

Kann ich Ihnen helfen?

Can I help you?

Ja, ich suche ein Hemd für meinen Mann.

Yes, I'm looking for a shirt for my husband.

Wir haben eine große Auswahl ... Möchte er ein gestreiftes oder vielleicht ein gemustertes Hemd?

There are a lot of choices here. Would he prefer a striped shirt or perhaps a patterned one?

Nein, lieber ein einfaches weißes Hemd.

No, I'd prefer a simple white shirt.

Da haben wir bestimmt etwas für Ihren Mann ... Ein schönes Leinenhemd. Was meinen Sie dazu?

Well, I'm quite sure we have something for your husband. A beautiful linen shirt. What do you think?

Oje! Das ist viel zu modern für ihn.

Oh dear, that's far too modern for him.

Ja, dann ...

Well, then...

1. DIALOGUE ACTIVITY

A. What does Julia want to buy?

B. What does she think about the one the salesclerk selects?

Use the following words and expressions to guide you through the lesson.

VOCABULARY

aus + sehen	to look like
die Auswahl (-en)	choice
bestimmt	definite, definitely
blau	blue
die Bluse (-n)	blouse
einfach	simple
empfehlen	to recommend
etwas	something
die Farbe (-n)	color
für (+ acc.)	for
gelb	yellow
gemustert	patterned
gestreift	striped
die Größe (-n)	size
grün	green
das Hemd (-en)	shirt
die Hose (-n)	pants
die Idee (-n)	idea
ihn	him (accusative object)
die Jacke (-n)	jacket
kennen	to know (a person)
das Leinenhemd (-en)	linen shirt
machen	to make, to do
modern	modern
na ja	well... (expresses doubt)
orange	orange
das Paar (-e)	pair
der Pullover (-)	sweater
der Rock (¨-e)	skirt
rosarot	pink
rot	red
schlank	slim
schlicht	simple, plain
schön	beautiful
die Seidenbluse (-n)	silk blouse
die Socke (-n)	sock
der Stil (-e)	style
suchen	to look for
viel	much
weiß	white
ziemlich	quite

2. ACTIVITY

Look at this color wheel: rotate the names so that they fit the colors.

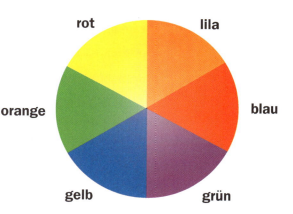

3. LISTENING ACTIVITY

 Herr and Frau Kerschner have lost their daughter Sabine while shopping in a department store. Can you help the store detective to find Sabine? Write down the colors of her hair and clothes.

1. **hair**

2. **jacket**

3. **sweater**

4. **skirt**

5. **shoes**

Frau Kerschner:	**Können Sie uns helfen? Wir haben unsere kleine Tochter verloren!**
Kaufhausdetektiv:	**Ja, natürlich. Wie alt ist sie?**
Herr Kerschner:	**Sie ist sechs Jahre alt.**
Kaufhausdetektiv:	**Und wie sieht sie aus? Ihre Haare?**
Frau Kerschner:	**Die sind kurz und dunkel.**
Kaufhausdetektiv:	**Ihre Jacke?**
Herr Kerschner:	**Die ist weiß und rot.**
Kaufhausdetektiv:	**Ihr Pullover?**
Frau Kerschner:	**Der ist orange.**
Herr Kerschner:	**Und ihr Rock ist blau.**
Frau Kerschner:	**Und Ihre Schuhe sind rot, mit weißen Socken.**
Kaufhausdetektiv:	**Sabine, sechs Jahre, dunkel, weiß, rot, blau ... gut! Warten Sie bitte. Und machen Sie sich keine Sorgen.**

4. LISTENING ACTIVITY

Listen to this dialogue between a shopper and a salesclerk. Can you fill in the missing information?

Kunde: Können Sie mir helfen? Ich suche eine [_____] für meine Frau.

Verkäuferin: Ja, natürlich. Suchen Sie einen bestimmten [_____] oder eine bestimmte [_____] ?

Kunde: Äh, das weiß ich nicht. Können Sie mir etwas empfehlen?

Verkäuferin: Na ja, ich kenne Ihre Frau nicht. Vielleicht eine schlichte [_____] Seidenbluse?

Kunde: Ja? ... Ja, das ist eine gute Idee.

Verkäuferin: Welche [_____] hat Ihre Frau?

Kunde: Das weiß ich nicht ... Sie ist ziemlich schlank.

Adjectives   GRAMMAR

If there is no article before the adjective and no noun after it, you just use the plain form (the form without an ending) of the adjective:

Der Rock ist rot.   The skirt is red.

But if the adjective comes in front of the noun, it takes an ending. Here are the endings in the nominative case (when the noun is the subject and is preceded by an article):

m.	*der rote Rock*	*ein roter Rock*
f.	*die rote Bluse*	*eine rote Bluse*
neuter	*das rote Hemd*	*ein rotes Hemd*
pl.	*die roten Hemden*	

5. READING ACTIVITY

Look again at these dialogues. Can you identify the adjectives? Underline them.

1

Verkäufer:	**Kann ich Ihnen helfen?**
Kundin:	**Ja, ich suche ein Hemd für meinen Mann.**
Verkäufer:	**Wir haben eine große Auswahl … Möchte er ein gestreiftes oder vielleicht ein gemustertes Hemd?**
Kundin:	**Nein, lieber ein einfaches weißes Hemd.**
Verkäufer:	**Da haben wir bestimmt etwas für Ihren Mann … Ein schönes Leinenhemd. Was meinen Sie dazu?**
Kundin:	**Oje! Das ist viel zu modern für ihn.**
Verkäufer:	**Ja, dann …**

2

Kunde:	**Können Sie mir helfen? Ich suche eine Bluse für meine Frau.**
Verkäuferin:	**Ja, natürlich. Suchen Sie einen bestimmten Stil oder eine bestimmte Farbe?**
Kunde:	**Äh, das weiß ich nicht. Können Sie mir etwas empfehlen?**
Verkäuferin:	**Na ja, ich kenne Ihre Frau nicht. Vielleicht eine schlichte weiße Seidenbluse?**
Kunde:	**Ja? … Ja, das ist eine gute Idee.**
Verkäuferin:	**Welche Größe hat Ihre Frau?**
Kunde:	**Das weiß ich nicht … Sie ist ziemlich schlank.**

6. WRITING ACTIVITY

Now fill in the correct endings in the blanks:

1

a. Ich suche einen weiß _____ Pullover.

b. Ich suche eine weiß _____ Bluse.

c. Ich suche ein weiß _____ Hemd.

2

a. Wir suchen einen schlicht _____ Rock.

b. Wir suchen eine schlicht _____ Jacke.

c. Wir suchen ein schlicht _____ Hemd.

3

a. Kann ich d _____ grün _____

Hose probieren?

b. Haben Sie rot _____ Röcke?

c. Das ist ein schön _____ Hemd.

7. **SPEAKING** **ACTIVITY** 66 99

These two people accidentally swapped shopping bags when they left the department store café. Now they're phoning the store to list the things they've lost. Can you complete their descriptions? All the words you need are in the box.

| orange   grünen   rosarote   grüne   gelben   rote   weiße   blaues |

Ich habe ein [   ] Hemd und eine

[   ] und [   ]

Unterhose und ein Paar grüne Socken verloren.

Ich habe einen [   ] Rock, eine

[   ] Bluse, einen [   ]

BH und eine [   ] und

[   ] Strumpfhose verloren.

8. SPEAKING ACTIVITY

You need help at a clothing store. Talk with the salesclerk.

Guten Tag. Sie wünschen?

Sie

Tell her you're looking for a pair of blue pants.

Welche Größe haben Sie?

Sie

Give your size.

Guten Tag. Kann ich Ihnen helfen?

Sie

Say you're looking for a green shirt.

Welche Größe haben Sie?

Sie

Give your size.

Check It!

Test what you've learned in this lesson and review anything you're not sure of.

CAN YOU . . . ?

name common items of clothing
der Pullover, die Bluse, das Hemd,
die Hose, der Rock

name colors
rot, blau, gelb, schwarz, weiß,
grün, braun

say you're looking for an item of a specific color
Ich suche eine blaue Hose/einen
blauen Rock.

BERLITZ HOTSPOT   Go to www.berlitzhotspot.com for...

Social Networking
Go to the **Berlitz Hotspot** and tell your friends what you are
wearing today!

Podcast 14
Shop til You Drop
Download the podcast.

Internet Activity
Are you interested in learning more about German fashion? Go to **Berlitz Hotspot** for links to some
German clothing brands. Look through the catalogues and identify the items you see by item type and
description (color, pattern, etc.). Say which items you want and what size and color you want them in.

Video 7 – The Clothing Shop
It's time to try on some clothes. How does the shopper ask the salesclerk for help? Do the clothes
fit well? Watch the video and learn how to find a fitting room and request clothes in another size.

Lesson 15

I'll Take the Small One.

Ich nehme den kleinen.

LESSON OBJECTIVES

Lesson 15 is about specifying the item you want. When you have completed this lesson, you'll know how to:

- identify what you want
- express opinions about items

DIALOGUE

Frau Armbruster has stopped at the information desk of *Karstadt*, a large department store with several floors, to ask where she can find a few items.

Können Sie mir bitte helfen? Ich suche ein Geschenk für meine kleine Nichte. Wo finde ich so etwas?

Can you help me, please? I'm looking for a present for my little niece. Where do I find something like that?

Im dritten Stock. Da ist die Spielwarenabteilung.

On the fourth floor. That's where the toy department is.

Und ich suche auch etwas für meinen Mann ... einen Fotoapparat vielleicht.

And I'm also looking for something for my husband... perhaps a camera.

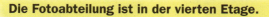

Die Fotoabteilung ist in der vierten Etage.

The photo department is on the fourth floor.

Ich möchte auch Parfüm kaufen. Wo ist die Parfümerie?

I'd like to buy some perfume as well. Where's the perfume department?

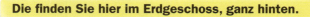

Die finden Sie hier im Erdgeschoss, ganz hinten.

It's located here on the first floor, at the very back.

152

Use the following words and expressions to guide you through the lesson.

VOCABULARY

Ausgezeichnet!	Excellent! Outstanding!	**Prima!**	Great!
das Auto (-s)	car	**die Puppe (-n)**	doll
beige	beige	**rosarot**	pink
braun	brown	**der Schlips (-e)**	tie
die Fotoabteilung (-en)	photography department	**schrecklich**	horrible
der Fotoapparat (-e)	camera	**schwarz**	black
das Geschenk (-e)	gift	**das Schweinchen (-)**	toy pig, little pig
das Geschoss (-e)	story, floor	**so etwas**	something like that
grau	gray	**die Spielwarenabteilung (-en)**	toy department
hässlich	ugly	**der Stock (-)/das Stockwerk (-e)**	story, floor
Igitt!	Yuck!	**der Teddy (-s)**	teddy bear
Klasse!	Great!	**Toll!**	Great!
klein	small	**weiß**	white
lila	purple	**Wie finden Sie das?**	What do you think of it?
mittelgroß	medium-sized	**Wunderschön!**	Lovely!
nehmen (er nimmt)	to take		
niedlich	cute		
das Parfüm (-s)	perfume		

1. DIALOGUE ACTIVITY

Whom does Frau Armbruster say she is looking for gifts for?

2. LISTENING ACTIVITY

 Listen to the dialogue again. Which floors are these departments on?

a. **the toy department**

b. **the photography department**

c. **perfumery**

3. SPEAKING ACTIVITY

You're showing a German visitor around a department store. He wants to know where to find certain items. Answer his questions, using *im … Stock, in der … Etage* or *im … Geschoss*. Note: Floor one in Germany is the second floor (US) or the first floor (UK).

Household Items and China	5
Photographic Equipment and Computers	4
Restaurant and Children's Clothes	3
Men's and Women's Fashions	2
Toys and Electrical Items	1
Cosmetics and Perfumery	G

Example: **Wo ist die Fotoabteilung?**
Im vierten Stock.
(Or: **In der vierten Etage./**
Im vierten Geschoss.)

a. **Wo sind die Haushaltswaren?**

b. **Wo kann ich einen Schlips kaufen?**

c. **Wo kann ich Parfüm für meine Frau kaufen?**

d. **Wo finde ich ein Geschenk für meinen kleinen Sohn?**

154

4. WRITING ACTIVITY

Here we are again at *Karstadt*. This time we're in the toy department: *die Spielwarenabteilung*. Herr Hartmann is buying toys for his children. *Teddys* (teddy bears), *Puppen* (dolls), *Schweinchen* (little pigs) and *Autos* (Cars), are all mentioned. Write down in German which items Herr Hartmann buys.

Example:

> *Er nimmt den kleinen Teddy, ...*

Herr Hartmann: **Was kosten die Teddys?**

Verkäuferin: **Der kleine 7€, der mittelgroße 16€ und der große 24€.**

Herr Hartmann: **Ich nehme den kleinen Teddy. Und was kosten die Puppen?**

Verkäuferin: **Die kleine 8€, die mittelgroße 15€ und die große 28€.**

Herr Hartmann: **Ja dann ... die mittelgroße ist schön. Ja, ich nehme die mittelgroße Puppe. Ach, und die Schweinchen! Sowas Niedliches! Was kosten sie?**

Verkäuferin: **6€.**

Herr Hartmann: **Ich nehme das rosarote. Was kosten diese Autos?**

Verkäuferin: **Die kleinen 4,50€, die mittelgroßen 7€ und die großen 10€.**

Herr Hartmann: **Dann nehme ich die kleinen Autos für 4,50€.**

5. **WRITING ACTIVITY**

Which of these expressions are positive (+), and which are negative (-)? Listen to the audio for help.

☐ **Ausgezeichnet!**   ☐ **Hässlich!**   ☐ **Igitt!**   ☐ **Prima!**

☐ **Klasse!**   ☐ **Schrecklich!**   ☐ **Toll!**   ☐ **Wunderschön!**

6. **SPEAKING ACTIVITY** 66 99

Use one of your new expressions in German to react to the following situations.

1. **Your sister shows you a new outfit that you think is really horrible.**

2. **Your friend tells you that he just got a raise at his job.**

3. **You see a shirt that you really like.**

4. **You eat a bite of food that has an awful taste.**

5. **You just get off work and your friend offers to take you out to dinner.**

6. **A good friend shows you a jacket in a store.**

7. **Your mom asks your opinion of a movie you just saw.**

8. **A close friend asks you how your day is going.**

PRONUNCIATION

Here's a chance to practice your pronunciation. Listen to the speaker and try to follow the same intonation.

One of the sounds in German that English speakers find most difficult is the *r*. Not only is the sound quite different from the English *r*, there are regional variations. In some areas, mostly in the south, the *r* is pronounced by vibrating the tip of the tongue:

rot

However, in most parts of Germany *r* is pronounced by vibrating the uvula, that little flap that hangs down at the back of your mouth:

rot   *rosarot*

Practice whenever you can. A nonsense phrase with a lot of *r*'s is:

das rosarote Rhinozeros   the pink rhinoceros

You may find it helpful to repeat this to yourself:

das rosarote Rhinozeros

When *r* comes at the end of a word it's pronounced as a vowel, rather like in British English "bitter:"

Bier   *hier*

GRAMMAR

The Cases

As you already know, articles can change according to the use of a noun. There are two object cases in German, the accusative and the dative. As a general rule, the direct object takes the accusative and the indirect object takes the dative.

	Nominative (subject)		Accusative		Dative	
m.	*der*	*ein*	*den*	*einen*	*dem*	*einem*
f.	*die*	*eine*	*die*	*eine*	*der*	*einer*
neut.	*das*	*ein*	*das*	*ein*	*dem*	*einem*
pl.	*die*		*die*	*die*	*den*	

7. READING ACTIVITY

We asked Peter: *Was wünschst du dir zum Geburtstag?* What do you want for your birthday? Read his response. (Note the informal is used because Peter is a friend.)

Wir: Peter, was wünschst du dir zum Geburtstag?

Peter: Also, bestimmt keine schöne Party oder große Torte oder so was. Geburtstagspartys gefallen mir nicht. Aber ein Handy ...? Oder vielleicht eine Digitalkamera? Hm, ja, das wäre nicht schlecht. Oder eine Reise nach Hawaii ... oder Südafrika?

What things does he not want?

What things would he like?

8. READING ACTIVITY

What would Anke and Rabea like for their birthdays? Read what they say and write down what they want in English.

Anke

Also ich wünsche mir einen Schrank voll Bücher.

Rabea

Hm, ich möchte Schokolade, viel Schokolade. Oder ein neues Auto.

9.   WRITING ACTIVITY

Now write down your wish list for a holiday or your birthday. *Use Ich wünsche mir ...* and the thing you want, in the accusative case. If you don't know all the words you need, consult your dictionary.

LEARNING TIP

When you're learning the words for clothes and for colors, try to picture the article or the color in your mind as you're saying the name. When you get dressed in the morning, see if you can say to yourself the German names of the items you're putting on, and their colors.

Check It!

Test what you've learned in this lesson and review anything you're not sure of.

CAN YOU . . . ?

☐ **say which item you want from a range**
Ich nehme den großen Teddy/die blaue Hose.

☐ **say what you think of something**
Toll!/Prima!/Wunderschön!
Hässlich!/Schrecklich!/Igitt!

Learn More ╋

Look up the German names of items aroun your home or office in a dictionary. Then wri out name tags in German and attach them to the items. (Remember to include *der/die das*.) Self-adhesive notes are ideal for this, they're easy to peel off.

BERLITZ HOTSPOT Go to www.berlitzhotspot.com for...

Social Networking
Go to **Berlitz Hotspot** and share your opinions on fashion with your Hotspot friends. Tell them which fashion items are your favorites. Try using some of your new vocabulary.

Podcast 15
Sizing
Download the podcast

Internet Activity
For more practice, return to the links to the German clothing websites at **Berlitz Hotspot** and give your opinions using your new expressions.

Lesson 16 By Train

Mit der Bahn

LESSON OBJECTIVES

Lesson 16 is about going to and from school or work. When you have completed this lesson, you'll know how to:

- talk about how you get to school or work
- say when you leave and arrive
- say how you prefer to travel and why

DIALOGUE

 Listen to these train announcements.

1

Intercity Nummer 503 nach Düsseldorf, planmäßige Abfahrt 11:07 Uhr auf Gleis acht.

Intercity number 503 to Düsseldorf, scheduled departure at 11:07 on platform eight.

2

Intercity Express Nummer 597 nach Magdeburg, planmäßige Abfahrt 11:40 Uhr auf Gleis sechs.

Intercity Express number 597 to Magdeburg, scheduled departure at 11:40 on platform six.

1. DIALOGUE ACTIVITY

What are the destinations for each train?

DID YOU KNOW?

German trains are fast, comfortable and reliable. The *Deutsche Bahn AG* is the national railway of Germany. It offers many domestic and international routes. Tickets can be purchased at the station (from a salesclerk or a ticketing machine), online or through a travel agent. Visit the website of Deutsche Bahn AG for schedules, fares and discounts.

DID YOU KNOW?

The *ICE, Intercity-Express; IC, Intercity*; and *EC, Eurocity*, are categories of express trains in Germany and nearby countries. Travelers may have to pay a surcharge, *Zuschlag*, in order to use them.

Use the following words and expressions to
guide you through the lesson.

ab (+ dat.)	from
ab + fahren	depart
die Abfahrt (-en)	departure
an + kommen	to arrive
auf (+ acc./dat.)	on
die Bahn (-en)	railroad, railway
bis	until, by
einfach	single, simple
einmal	once
fahren (er fährt)	to go (by vehicle)
die Fahrkarte (-n)	ticket (for travel)
das Gleis (-e)	rail, platform
hin und zurück	round trip
die Klasse (-n)	class

die Minute (-n)	minute
müssen (ich muss, er muss)	to have to
planmäßig	scheduled
planmäßige Abfahrt	scheduled (time of) departure
um + steigen	to change (trains, etc.)
Wie komme ich am besten dorthin?	What's the best way for me to get there?
der Zug (¨-e)	train
der Zuschlag (-schläge)	supplement
zweimal	twice

2. LISTENING ACTIVITY

Listen to the announcements. Write the number of each announcement under the corresponding information board.

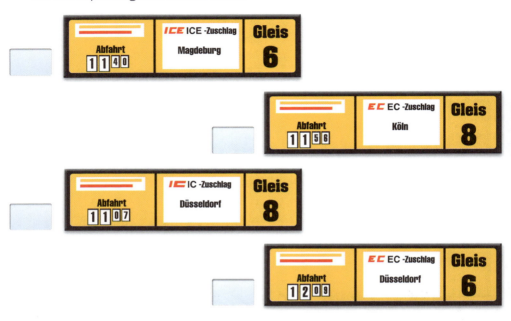

1   **Intercity Nummer 503 nach Düsseldorf, planmäßige Abfahrt 11:07 Uhr auf Gleis acht.**

2   **Intercity Express Nummer 597 nach Magdeburg, planmäßige Abfahrt 11:40 Uhr auf Gleis sechs.**

3   **Eurocity Nummer 109 nach Düsseldorf, planmäßige Abfahrt 12:09 Uhr auf Gleis sechs.**

4   **Eurocity Nummer 46 nach Köln, planmäßige Abfahrt 11:56 Uhr auf Gleis acht.**

3. WRITING ACTIVITY

Write a text message to your friend to let her know what time you will be leaving. Here's the relevant information: Euro City Number 32 to Berlin with a scheduled departure at 12:10 on platform 7.

4. LISTENING ACTIVITY

Which of the following tickets does each speaker ask for? (Some of the tickets are not asked for at all.) Circle your answers.

a. **a one-way ticket to Bremen**

b. **a round-trip ticket to Bremen**

c. **two round-trip tickets to Mannheim**

d. **a round-trip ticket to Mannheim**

e. **two one-way tickets to Mannheim**

f. **two one-way tickets to Vienna**

g. **two round-trip tickets to Vienna**

h. **a round-trip ticket to Vienna**

5. 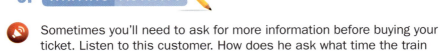 **WRITING ACTIVITY**

Sometimes you'll need to ask for more information before buying your ticket. Listen to this customer. How does he ask what time the train leaves and from which platform? Complete the answers to the questions.

a. **Um wie viel Uhr fährt der Zug? Der Zug fährt ...**

b. **Wo muss man umsteigen? Man muss ...**

c. **Was kostet die Fahrt insgesamt? Die Fahrt ...**

d. **Was kostet der Zuschlag? Der Zuschlag ...**

e. **Wo fährt der Zug ab? Der Zug fährt ...**

Kunde:	**Ich muss bis 19:30 Uhr in Freiburg im Breisgau sein. Wie komme ich am besten dorthin?**
Bahnangestellter:	**Sie nehmen den ICE 595 bis Mannheim und steigen dann in den IC 603 um. Sie kommen um 19:02 Uhr in Freiburg an.**
Kunde:	**Wann fährt der Zug?**
Bahnangestellter:	**In 20 Minuten, um 11:46 Uhr.**
Kunde:	**Gut. Dann einmal nach Freiburg, einfach, bitte.**
Bahnangestellter:	**Erste oder zweite Klasse?**
Kunde:	**Zweite Klasse.**
Bahnangestellter:	**117€ plus 20€ ICE-Zuschlag macht 137€ insgesamt.**
Kunde:	**Bitte schön. Wo fährt der Zug ab?**
Bahnangestellter:	**Auf Gleis zwei. Hier ist Ihre Fahrkarte. Gute Reise!**
Kunde:	**Danke. Wiedersehen.**

Fahren and Gehen

GRAMMAR

You've already encountered *gehen*, "to go (on foot)." *Fahren* is always used when travel by vehicle is implied.

6. WRITING ACTIVITY

Look at this ticket, then fill in the blanks in the conversation.

Beamter: **Bitte schön?**

Sie: **Einmal** _____ **.**

Beamter: **Erste oder zweite Klasse?**

Sie: _____ **.**

Beamter: **Fahren Sie mit dem ICE oder mit dem EC?**

Sie: _____ **.**

Beamter: **Das macht dann einundfünfzig Euro inklusive ICE-Zuschlag.**

7. SPEAKING ACTIVITY

How would you buy these tickets? Prepare your answers, then listen to the dialogues and follow the prompts.

a. **You are traveling from Hamburg to Berlin. You want a round-trip ticket for two people, second class.**

b. **You are traveling from Cologne (Köln) to Frankfurt. You want a one-way ticket for one person, first class.**

Bahnangestellte:	**Bitte schön?**
Sie:	Ask for a round-trip ticket to Berlin for two.
Bahnangestellte:	**Erste oder zweite Klasse?**
Sie:	Second class.
Bahnangestellte:	**Fahren Sie mit dem ICE oder mit dem D-Zug?**
Sie:	With the ICE.
Bahnangestellte:	**Das macht dann 114€.**
Sie:	Ask what time the train leaves.
Bahnangestellte:	**Der nächste Zug fährt um 13:05 Uhr auf Gleis 4 ab.**
Sie:	Say thanks and goodbye.

Bahnangestellte:	**Bitte schön?**
Sie:	Ask for a one-way ticket to Frankfurt for one.
Bahnangestellte:	**Erste oder zweite Klasse?**
Sie:	First class.
Bahnangestellte:	**Fahren Sie mit dem ICE oder mit dem D-Zug?**
Sie:	With the ICE.
Bahnangestellte:	**Das macht dann 69€.**
Sie:	What time does the train leave?
Bahnangestellte:	**Um 17:05 Uhr auf Gleis 12.**
Sie:	Say thanks and goodbye.
Bahnangestellte:	**Nichts zu danken. Auf Wiedersehen.**

Adjective Endings, Nominative Case   **GRAMMAR**

After *der/die* (singular)/*das,* adjectives always take the ending *-e:*

der letzte Bus   die letzte U-Bahn   das letzte Auto
the last bus/subway/car

After *die* (plural), adjectives always take the ending *-en:*

die letzten Busse

DID YOU KNOW?

Most German towns and cities have an efficient and comprehensive public transportation system. The larger cities have buses, a *Straßenbahn* network, a *U-Bahn* network and an *S-Bahn* network. For the *U-Bahn* and the *S-Bahn,* you have to buy your ticket before boarding the train; for buses, you can buy tickets in advance or most of the times from the driver, and some streetcars or trams have ticket vending machines on board, as well as at the stops.

DID YOU KNOW?

Nichts zu danken literally means "nothing to thank." It's a common expression you can use when someone thanks you for something. Or you can just say:

Bitte, bitte schön, bitte sehr, or more casually: *Bitte, bitte.*

Check It!

Test what you've learned in this lesson and review anything you're not sure of.

CAN YOU . . . ?

☐ **ask for a single ticket for one person to Bremen**
Einmal Bremen, einfach, bitte.

☐ **ask for a round-trip ticket for two to Hanover**
Zweimal Hannover, hin und zurück, bitte.

☐ **ask for recommendations about how to get to a place**
Wie komme ich am besten dorthin?

☐ **ask when the train leaves**
Wann fährt der Zug?

BERLITZ HOTSPOT   Go to www.berlitzhotspot.com for...

Social Networking
Do you have a lot of experience using trains? Have you ever traveled on one through a German-speaking country? Go to **Berlitz Hotspot** and tell your Hotspot friends about your experiences and share any handy tips you have.

Podcast 16
Die Bahnen
Download the podcast.

Internet Activity
Are you interested in more practice regarding trains? Go to **Berlitz Hotspot** to access links to rail sytems in German-speaking Europe. See if you can negotiate your way through the sites as if you were going to purchase tickets.

Video 8 – Commuting to Work
A businessman takes public transportation to work. What is his routine? How long does the commute take? Watch the video and learn about the weekday commute.

Ein Auto mieten

LESSON OBJECTIVES

Lesson 17 is about renting a car. When you have completed this lesson, you'll know how to:

- rent a car
- differentiate between permission, obligation and prohibition

DIALOGUE

 Listen as a customer rents a car.

Kundin:	**Ich möchte ein Auto mieten. Haben Sie eine Preisliste?**
	I'd like to rent a car. Do you have a price list?

Kundenbetreuerin:	**Ja natürlich. Bitte schön.**
	Yes, of course. Here you are.

Kundin:	**Danke. Ich möchte einen VW Polo oder einen ähnlichen Kleinwagen. Haben Sie so etwas?**
	Thank you. I would like a VW Polo or a similar small car. Do you have anything like that?

Kundenbetreuerin:	**Ja, haben wir. Das wäre Preisklasse B.**
	Yes we do. That would be price class B.

Kundin:	**Ich brauche den Wagen für drei Tage ab heute.**
	I need the car for three days from today.

Kundenbetreuerin:	**Kein Problem. Ich brauche Ihren Führerschein und eine Kreditkarte.**
	No problem. I need your driver's license and a credit card.

1. DIALOGUE ACTIVITY

A. What type of car does the customer want to rent?

B. When does she want the car?

172

Use the following words and expressions to guide you through the lesson.

VOCABULARY

ab + biegen	to turn off	der Kombi (-s)	station wagon
ab + steigen	to get off, dismount	die Kreditkarte (-n)	credit card
ähnlich	similar	die Limousine (-n)	sedan (car)
an + halten	to stop (in car)	mieten	to hire; rent
das Auto (-s)	car	mittlerer/e/es	medium-sized
die Begrenzung (-en)	limit, border	parken	to park
beide	both	die Parkgebühr (-en)	parking fee
brauchen	to need	die Parkuhr (-en)	parking meter
die Einbahnstraße (-n)	one-way street	die Preisklasse (-n)	price class
[r]ein + fahren	to turn in, enter	die Preisliste (-n)	price list
der Fahrzeugtyp (-en)	type of vehicle	das Problem (-e)	problem
der Führerschein (-e)	driver's license	Rad fahren	to cycle
die Geldbuße (-n)	fine	das Schild (-er)	sign
die Haftpflichtver-sicherung (-en)	liability insurance	die Versicherung (-en)	insurance
Halt!	Stop!	der Wagen (-)	car
heute	today	Was ist los?	What's the matter?
der Kleinwagen (-)	small car	Was machen Sie da?	What are you doing (there)?
		Wie lange?	How long?

2. LISTENING ACTIVITY

Listen again to the dialogue and to another customer who wants to rent a car. What will the total price be for each of the customers?

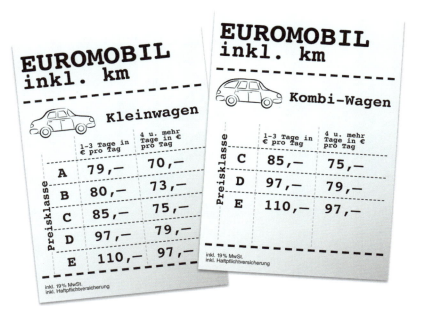

EUROMOBIL inkl. km

Kleinwagen

Preisklasse	1-3 Tage in € pro Tag	4 u. mehr Tage in € pro Tag
A	79,—	70,—
B	80,—	73,—
C	85,—	75,—
D	97,—	79,—
E	110,—	97,—

inkl. 19% MwSt.
inkl. Haftpflichtversicherung

EUROMOBIL inkl. km

Kombi-Wagen

Preisklasse	1-3 Tage in € pro Tag	4 u. mehr Tage in € pro Tag
C	85,—	75,—
D	97,—	79,—
E	110,—	97,—

inkl. 19% MwSt.
inkl. Haftpflichtversicherung

1

Kundin:	Ich möchte ein Auto mieten. Haben Sie eine Preisliste?
Kundenbetreuerin:	Ja natürlich. Bitte schön.
Kundin:	Danke. Ich möchte einen VW Polo oder einen ähnlichen Kleinwagen. Haben Sie so etwas?
Kundenbetreuerin:	Ja, haben wir. Das wäre Preisklasse B.
Kundin:	Ich brauche den Wagen für drei Tage ab heute.
Kundenbetreuerin:	Kein Problem. Ich brauche Ihren Führerschein und eine Kreditkarte.

2

Kunde:	Wir möchten einen großen Kombi für 14 Tage.
Kundenbetreuerin:	Wir haben einen Volvo und einen Opel. Beide sind Preisklasse E.
Kundin:	Ist das Kilometergeld inbegriffen?
Kundenbetreuerin:	Ja, und auch die Haftpflichtversicherung.
Kunde:	Gut, nehmen wir dann den Volvo?
Kundin:	Ja, ist mir recht.
Kundenbetreuerin:	Werden Sie beide fahren? Dann brauche ich beide Führerscheine und eine Kreditkarte.

3. SPEAKING ACTIVITY

Rent a medium-sized station wagon, *einen mittleren Kombi,* for seven days. Prepare what you'd say, then listen to the dialogue and follow the prompts.

Kundenbetreuerin:	**Bitte schön?**
Sie:	Say you would like to rent a medium-sized station wagon.
Kundenbetreuerin:	**Das wäre Preisklasse D. Für wie lange möchten Sie den Wagen mieten?**
Sie:	Say for seven days.
Kundenbetreuerin:	**Kein Problem. Ich brauche Ihren Führerschein und eine Kreditkarte.**
Sie:	Say: Here you are. Ask if the mileage is included.
Kundenbetreuerin:	**Ja, das Kilometergeld ist inbegriffen.**

(nicht) müssen and *(nicht) dürfen*

GRAMMAR

To say that someone must do something, use *müssen*. To say that someone may (i.e., is permitted to) do something, use *dürfen*.

Sie müssen anhalten.	You must stop.
Sie dürfen anhalten.	You may stop.

To say that someone must not do something, use *nicht dürfen*.

Watch out: *Sie müssen nicht* means "you don't have to." It doesn't mean "you must not."

Sie dürfen nicht anhalten.	You must not stop.
Sie müssen nicht anhalten (aber Sie dürfen).	You don't have to stop (but you may).

Modal Verbs

Verbs that are used with another verb to modify its meaning are called modal verbs. For example, *müssen*, "to have to", *dürfen*, "to be permitted to", and *können*, "to be able to", are usually used as modal verbs. When a modal verb is used, the other verb goes to the end of the sentence. The infinitive form of that verb is used. Compare these two sentences:

Ich parke in der Uhlandstraße.
I park in Uhlandstraße.

Ich muss/darf/kann in der Uhlandstraße parken.
I must/may/can park in Uhlandstraße.

The German literally says: "I must in the Uhlandstraße park."

4. LISTENING ACTIVITY

Driving around town can be hazardous. Here's a policeman who's having a difficult time keeping the motorists in line. Decide whether the policeman is expressing permission, obligation and/or prohibition in each case.

1 Polizist: **Halt! Was machen Sie da?**

Mann: **Äh ... wie bitte?**

Polizist: **Hier dürfen Sie nicht reinfahren. Das ist eine Einbahnstraße.**

Mann: **Oh, Entschuldigung!**

Polizist: **Ihren Führerschein, bitte.**

2 Polizist: **Steigen Sie bitte ab.**

Frau: **Ja warum denn?**

Polizist: **Hier darf man nicht Rad fahren.**

Frau: **Oh! Entschuldigung.**

3 Polizist: **Halt!**

Mann: **Was ist los?**

Polizist: **Sehen Sie das Schild? Sie müssen hier anhalten.**

4 Frau: **Entschuldigen Sie, darf ich hier parken?**

Polizist: **Ja, Sie dürfen. Aber Sie müssen eine Parkgebühr zahlen. Da vorn ist die Parkuhr.**

Separable Verbs

There are many separable verbs relating to travel and transport (*ankommen, absteigen*, etc.). If you use an auxiliary verb with a separable verb, remember to use the infinitive form of the separable verb, and put it at the end of the sentence:

Ich biege rechts ein.	I turn to the right.
Ich muss rechts einbiegen.	I must turn to the right.

5. WRITING ACTIVITY

Complete these sentences with *darf* or *muss*, as most appropriate.

1. **Hier** [   ] **man rechts abbiegen.**

2. **Hier** [   ] **man anhalten.**

3. **Hier** [   ] **man nicht über 30 fahren.**

4. **Hier** [   ] **man nicht Rad fahren.**

6. LISTENING ACTIVITY

Listen to Arne interviewing some of the employees at Transpress about how they get to work, then circle the following statements that are correct.

a. Alle Leute fahren mit dem Auto zur Arbeit.

b. Keiner fährt mit dem Zug zur Arbeit.

c. Im Sommer fahren viele mit der Straßenbahn ins Büro.

d. Zwei Frauen bringen ihre Kinder zur Schule.

e. Eine Frau nimmt ihre Kinder mit, weil sie Lehrerin ist.

f. Alle Frauen fahren alleine zur Arbeit.

Arne: Wie kommen Sie zur Arbeit?

Frau: Ich fahre mit dem Auto.

Arne: Wie lange fahren Sie?

Frau: Circa 25 Minuten.

Arne: Wie weit ist es?

Frau: Ungefähr zehn Kilometer.

Arne: Fahren Sie allein?

Frau: Nein, ich bringe erst meine Tochter zur Schule.

Arne: Wie kommen Sie jeden Tag zur Arbeit?

Mann: Mit dem Auto.

Arne: Und wie lange fahren Sie?

Mann: Ich brauche circa eine Stunde im Berufsverkehr.

Arne: Fahren Sie allein?

Mann: Ja, ich fahre allein.

Arne: Wie kommen Sie zur Arbeit?

Frau: Mit dem Auto.

Arne: Wie lange fahren Sie zur Arbeit?

Frau: Eine Stunde.

Arne: Wie weit ist es?

Frau: Nur 30 Kilometer, aber es gibt oft Staus.

Arne: Fahren Sie allein?

Frau: Nein, ich bringe morgens erst meine Kinder zur Schule.

Arne: Wie kommen Sie zur Arbeit?

Mann: Jeden Tag mit dem PKW.

Arne: Wie lange fahren Sie zur Arbeit?

Mann: Manchmal nur zehn Minuten; bei Stau eine Stunde.

Arne: Wie weit ist es?

Mann: Ungefähr fünf Kilometer.

Arne: Fahren Sie allein?

Mann: Ja.

7. READING ACTIVITY

Your friend Sandra sent you a message telling you how to get to her house.
Check your map and see if you can say which street she lives on.

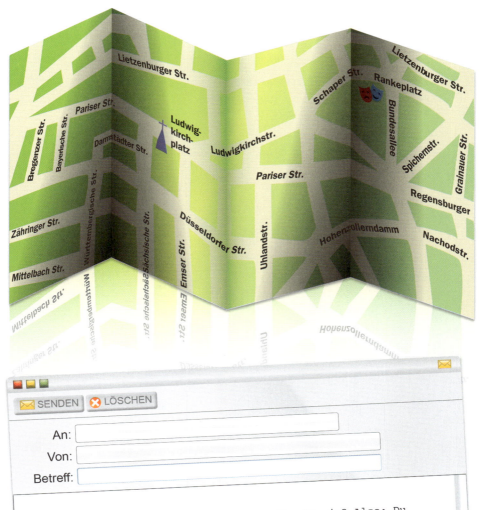

Check It!

Test what you've learned in this lesson and review anything you're not sure of.

CAN YOU . . . ?

☐ **say you would like to rent a car for...days**
Ich möchte ein Auto für sieben Tage mieten.

☐ **say that someone may/must do something**
Sie dürfen/müssen hier parken.

☐ **say that someone mustn't/need not do something**
Sie dürfen/müssen hier nicht parken.

BERLITZ HOTSPOT   Go to www.berlitzhotspot.com for...

 Social Networking
Have you driven around Europe or in a German-speaking country?
Go to **Berlitz Hotspot** and share your experiences.

 Podcast 17
Rules of the Road
Download the podcast.

 Internet Activity
Are you interested in more practice? Use your favorite search engine to access car rental websites in German. Based on their offers, create dialogues of you renting a car.

Lesson 18 In the City

In der Großstadt

LESSON OBJECTIVES

Lesson 18 is about getting around using public transportation. When you have completed this lesson, you'll know how to:

- understand and give directions for public transportation
- ask and say how often a service runs

DIALOGUE

Listen to this tourist asking for directions.

Entschuldigen Sie, wie komme ich zur Museumsinsel?

Excuse me, how do I get to Museumsinsel?

Fahren Sie mit der S1 Richtung Oranienburg bis "Unter den Linden." Das sind drei Haltestellen. Von dort können Sie zu Fuß gehen. Hm ... das dauert eine Viertelstunde. Oder Sie können den Bus nehmen.

Take the S1 towards Oranienburg until Unter den Linden. That's three stops. From there you can walk. Well... it takes a quarter of an hour. Or you can take the bus.

1. DIALOGUE ACTIVITY

A. **Where does the tourist want to go?**

B. **Does it sound nearby or far away?**

Use the following words and expressions to guide you through the lesson.

VOCABULARY

abends	in the evening(s)	**der Platz (¨-e)**	square
alle … Minuten	every…minutes	**die Richtung (-en)**	direction
aus + steigen	to get out	**Richtung Vinetastraße**	(in the) direction (of) Vinetastraße
der Bahnhof (-höfe)	(train) station	**die S-Bahn (-en)**	urban light railway
die Brücke (-n)	bridge	**(= Schnellbahn)**	
der Bus (-se)	bus	**die Straßenbahn (-en)**	tram, trolley bus, streetcar
dauern	to last	**die U-Bahn (-en)**	subway
ein + werfen	insert	**(= Untergrundbahn)**	
der Fahrschein (-e)	ticket (for bus, etc.)	**um + steigen**	to change (trains, etc.)
Das dauert eine Viertelstunde.	It takes a quarter of an hour.	**die Viertelstunde (-n)**	quarter of an hour
das Geld	money	**Von dort können Sie zu Fuß gehen.**	From there you can walk (go on foot).
die Großstadt (-städte)	metropolitan area	**wählen**	to select
halber/e/es	half	**das Wechselgeld**	change (money)
im (= in dem)	in the (m., neuter)	**weit**	far
die Insel (-n)	island	**der Zoo (-s)**	zoo
jeder/e/es	every, each	**zu Fuß**	on foot
letzter/e/es	last	**zur (= zu der)**	to the (f.)
die Linie (-n)	line		
oft	often		

DID YOU KNOW?

Museumsinsel, Museum Island, is the name of a group of internationally acclaimed museums located on an island in the Spree River, Berlin. *Museumsinsel* is a UNESCO World Heritage site.

185

2. LISTENING ACTIVITY

Listen to the audio and follow along on the map. How many stops will the tourists have to travel to reach these places from Yorckstraße Station?

BERLIN U-Bahn

Tiergarten

Hansaplatz

Richtung Spandau

Fried

Bellevue   Lehrter Stadtbahnhof

Zoologischer Garten

Unter den Linden

Wittenberg-platz

Nollendorf-platz

Potsdamer Platz

U3

Kurfürsten-damm

U2   U4   Kurfüstenstr.

Anha

M

Gleisdreieck

Augsburger Str.

Bülowstr.

S1

Richtung Uhlandstraße

Spichernstr.

Yorckstr.   Yor

Güntzelstr.

Viktoria-Luise-Platz

Berliner Str.

a. **der Zoo**

b. **das Nikolaiviertel** (the Nikolai Quarter)

c. **der Kurfürstendamm** or **der Ku'damm**

1

Frau: **Entschuldigung, wie komme ich zum Zoo?**

Mann: **Fahren Sie mit der S1 Richtung Oranienburg bis Potsdamer Platz. Steigen Sie dort in die U2 Richtung Spandau um. Das sind sieben Haltestellen.**

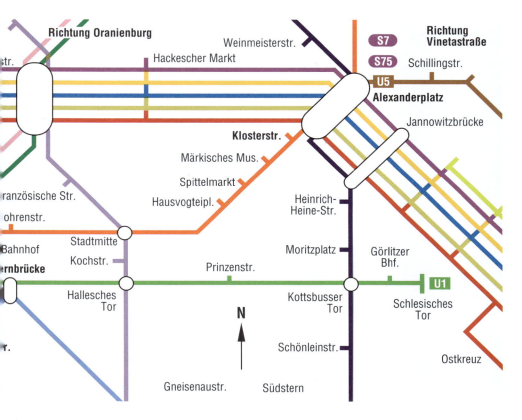

Richtung Oranienburg

Weinmeisterstr.

Hackescher Markt

str.

S7

S75   Schillingstr.

Richtung Vinetastraße

U5

Alexanderplatz

Jannowitzbrücke

Klosterstr.

Märkisches Mus.

Spittelmarkt

ranzösische Str.

Hausvogteipl.

ohrenstr.

Heinrich-Heine-Str.

Bahnhof

Stadtmitte

Kochstr.

rnbrücke

Prinzenstr.

Moritzplatz

Görlitzer Bhf.

U1

r.

Hallesches Tor

N

Kottsbusser Tor

Schlesisches Tor

Schönleinstr.

Ostkreuz

Gneisenaustr.

Südstern

2

Frau 1: **Entschuldigung, können Sie mir helfen? Wie komme ich zum Nikolaiviertel?**

Frau 2: **Steigen Sie am Potsdamer Platz in die U2 Richtung Vinetastraße um. Fahren Sie bis Klosterstraße, dann steigen Sie aus. Von dort aus müssen Sie zu Fuß gehen. Es ist nicht weit. Das sind acht Haltestellen.**

3

Mann 1: **Entschuldigen Sie, wie komme ich zum Kurfürstendamm?**

Mann 2: **Zum Ku'damm? Fahren Sie bis Potsdamer Platz und steigen Sie dort in die U2 Richtung Spandau um. Steigen Sie am Gleisdreieck in die U1 Richtung Uhlandstraße. Das sind sieben Haltestellen.**

3. SPEAKING ACTIVITY

 You're at Alexanderplatz. You're asked how to get to the following places:

a. Bahnhof Zoo (Zoologischer Garten)

b. Wittenbergplatz

c. Unter den Linden

Can you give directions to these tourists?

Entschuldigen Sie, wie komme ich zum Bahnhof Zoo?

Tell him to take the U2 towards Spandau.

Entschuldigung, wie komme ich zum Wittenbergplatz?

Take the U2 towards Spandau.

Wie komme ich zu Unter den Linden?

Take the U2 towards Spandau until Potsdamer Platz. Then take the S1 towards Oranienburg.

DID YOU KNOW?

 Most larger German towns and cities have a comprehensive public transportation system, consisting of: *der Bus* (bus), *die Straßenbahn* (tram), *die U-Bahn* (subway or underground) and *die Schnellbahn* or *S-Bahn* (an express or street level railway).

Contracted Forms

Notice that *in dem* is usually written and pronounced *im*. Other contracted forms that you'll see: *zu + dem = zum, zu + der = zur.*

4. LISTENING ACTIVITY

Write down the bus schedule that matches each dialogue.

A.	06	Uhr	00	20	40			
	07	Uhr	00	20	40			
B.	14	Uhr	05	15	25	35	45	55
	15	Uhr	05	15	25	35	45	55
C.	22	Uhr	12	27	42	57		
	23	Uhr	12	42				
D.	06	Uhr	45					
	07	Uhr	15	45				

1

Mann 1:	**Wann fährt der letzte Bus nach Potsdam?**
Mann 2:	**Abends um 11:42 Uhr.**

2

Mann:	**Wie oft fährt der Bus Richtung Oranienburg?**
Frau:	**Alle zehn Minuten.**

3

Frau:	**Wie oft fährt die Linie 1?**
Mann:	**Alle 15 Minuten.**
Frau:	**Wann fährt der nächste Bus?**
Mann:	**Um 22:42 Uhr.**

4

Mann:	**Wie oft fährt der Bus Richtung Dahlem?**
Frau:	**Jede halbe Stunde.**
Mann:	**Wann fährt der erste Bus?**
Frau:	**Um viertel vor sieben.**

5

Mann:	**Wann fährt der nächste Bus nach Dahlem?**
Frau:	**Um 7:45 Uhr.**

6

Frau 1:	**Wie oft fahren die Busse zur Universität?**
Frau 2:	**Alle 20 Minuten.**
Frau 1:	**Und wann fährt der erste Bus?**
Frau 2:	**Um sechs Uhr.**

5. SPEAKING ACTIVITY

Look at the schedules again and say in German how often each bus runs.

A.	06	Uhr	00	20	40			
	07	Uhr	00	20	40			
B.	14	Uhr	05	15	25	35	45	55
	15	Uhr	05	15	25	35	45	55
C.	22	Uhr	12	27	42	57		
	23	Uhr	12	42				
D.	06	Uhr	45					
	07	Uhr	15	45				

6. READING ACTIVITY

On official notices, instructions are often expressed with infinitives. Match these illustrations of public transportation to the instructions below.

a.

b.

c.

d.

Wechselgeld und Fahrschein entnehmen.

Fahrschein im Bus entwerten.

Geld einwerfen.

Fahrschein wählen.

PRONUNCIATION

Two sounds that can be a little difficult for English speakers to pronounce are *ch* as in *ich* and *ch* as in *ach*. The *ach* sound is pronounced at the back of the throat, like the *ch* sound in the Scottish word "loch."

Ach!
nach
Sprache

The *ich* sound, on the other hand, is pronounced by putting the tip of the tongue behind your lower front teeth, spreading your lips and breathing out quite hard to produce a hissing sound like this: –*ch*.

ich
mich
spreche

And now the two sounds together.

ich – ach
mich – nach
spreche – Sprache

The *ich* sound always comes after *e, i, ü, ö* and *ä*:

spreche
spricht
Sprüche

The *ach* sound always comes after *a, o, u*:

Sprache
gesprochen
Spruch

It may take you some time to get the pronunciation right, but don't lose heart and keep on practising. If you find it difficult, here's some consolation: In Swiss German they don't have the *ich* sound.

Adjective Endings

As you know, adjectives take an ending when they come in front of the noun. The endings differ, depending on which article is used. You've already seen the endings with the indefinite article. The endings with the definite article are simpler—adjectives always end in -e or -en:

Accusative		Dative	
den blauen Rock	the blue skirt	im ersten Stock	on the first floor
die blaue Bluse	the blue blouse	in der ersten Etage	on the first floor
das blaue Hemd	the blue shirt	im ersten Geschoss	on the first floor
die blauen Hemden	the blue shirts	in den ersten Etagen	on the first floors

8. WRITING ACTIVITY

Can you fill in the correct endings of the adjectives?

a. Ich kaufe das rot_____ Auto.

b. Im erst_____ Stock ist die Drogerie.

c. Ich möchte eine grün_____ Bluse und weiß_____ Socken.

d. Paula nimmt die halb_____ Portion Pommes und ein ganz_____ Brot.

e. Die klein_____ Puppe trägt ein gelb_____ Kleid und der groß_____ Teddy ein braun_____.

f. Clara und Paul haben beide blau_____ Augen.

g. Ich habe einen ähnlich_____ Pullover.

h. Herr Marten trägt das schwarz_____ Jackett.

Word Order

GRAMMAR

In previous lessons you saw that word order can be changed for emphasis, as long as the verb comes second in the sentence. It's important to realize though that the verb doesn't have to be the second word in the sentence, it has to be the second expression. For example, a noun with its article and an adjective describing the noun counts as one expression. So in the sentence:

Der letzte Bus fährt um elf.   The last bus goes at eleven.

the phrase *der letzte Bus* is the first expression, and *fährt* is the second expression.

Look at these sentences:

Von dort können Sie zu Fuß gehen.   From there you can walk (go on foot).
Sie können von dort zu Fuß gehen.   You can walk from there.

Von dort is one expression, so *können* is the second expression in both of these sentences.

LEARNING TIP

When listening to recordings in German, do your best to imitate the exact rhythm and intonation of the speakers. If you can reproduce the rhythm and intonation accurately, other pronunciation errors, such as mispronouncing certain sounds, will not be as noticeable and your German will be easier to understand.

193

Check It!

Test what you've learned in this lesson and review anything you're not sure of.

CAN YOU . . . ?

☐ **give directions on how to get to a place by public transportation**
Fahren Sie mit der S1 bis Potsdamer Platz.
Steigen Sie in die U2 (Richtung Vinetastraße) um.

☐ **ask how often a service runs**
Wie oft fahren die Busse/fährt die U-Bahn?

☐ **say how often a service runs**
Die Busse fahren alle zwanzig Minuten/jede halbe Stunde.
Die U-Bahn fährt alle zehn Minuten/jede Viertelstunde.

Learn More

Get a hold of some street, subway and bus maps for cities in German-speaking countries. Study the names of the major sights you'd like to visit, the streets on which they are located and the major subway stations. Practice using the language you'd need to travel on public transportation to and from different places.

BERLITZ HOTSPOT

Go to www.berlitzhotspot.com for...

Social Networking
What's your experience using public transport abroad? Go to **Berlitz Hotspot** and share your experiences.

Podcast 18
Out and About
Download the podcast

Internet Activity
Are you interested in more practice? Use your favorite search engine to access rail maps for large German-speaking cities, for example, Hamburg, Zürich, Berlin, etc. Practice explaining how to get from place to place using your new vocabulary.

Video 9 – Taxi!
A woman needs a taxi. How does she hail a taxi? Where is she going? Watch the video and find out one way to get a taxi in Germany.

Test 2 | Review of Lessons 10-18

1. Can you complete the word grid? All the clues are related to travel and transportation. Write the answers in capital letters (use ss instead of ß.)

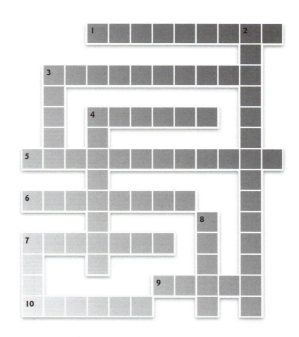

Across

1. to change (trains etc.) **(9)**

3. ticket **(10)**

4. hin und **(6)**

5. insurance **(12)**

6. direction **(8)**

7. departure **(7)**

9. der Zug nach Mannheim fährt auf ... 3 ab. **(5)**

10. once **(6)**

Down

2. Hier dürfen Sie nur in eine Richtung fahren. **(14)**

3. Ich ... nach Köln. **(5)**

4. supplement **(8)**

7. Die Busse fahren ... zehn Minuten. **(4)**

8. to go (on foot) **(5)**

2. How would you ask for these items in a store? Start each sentence with *Ich suche ...*

Example: **Ich suche eine blaue Hose.**

a. **red skirt**

b. **green pants**

c. **black jacket**

d. **white shirt**

e. **blue pullover**

3. Can you assign each of the items to the correct department of the store?

Parfüm

Brot

Schlips

Kugelschreiber

Rock

Puppe

Bluse

Herrenhose

Teddy

COMPUTER

Fleisch

ETAGENPLAN	
Dachterrasse:	Café
2 Etage:	Elektrogeräte Spielwaren Schreibwaren
1 Etage:	Sportartikel Herrenmode
Erdgeschoss:	Damenmode Kosmetika Lebensmittel

4. This dialogue has been scrambled. Can you put the words in the correct order?

Empfangschef:	**. Guten Tag ? etwas für ich Kann Sie tun**
Gast:	**. Ja . Doppelzimmer Dusche ein mit möchten Wir**
Empfangschef:	**? bleiben lange möchten Sie Wie**
Gast:	**. bleiben drei möchten Nächte Wir**
Empfangschef:	**, . Doppelzimmer ein frei haben Ja wir . Das kostet Euro Nacht pro einhundertzehn**
Gast:	**? Frühstück inbegriffen Ist**
Empfangschef:	**, . Frühstück inbegriffen ist Ja**
Gast:	**. es nehmen Wir**
Empfangschef:	**. aus bitte das Formular Füllen Sie**

Empfangschef:

Gast:

Empfangschef:

Gast:

Empfangschef:

Gast:

Empfangschef:

Gast:

Empfangschef:

5. Answer each of the questions with full sentences, using the time shown on the clockface. Where times are shown in the 24-hour clock, answer using the 24-hour clock also.

Example:

 Wie spät ist es?   **Es ist halb sieben.**

 Wann fährt der Zug?   **Der Zug fährt um achtzehn Uhr dreißig.**

a.

b.

c.   d.   e.

a.   **Wie spät ist es?**

b.   **Wie lange ist die Bibliothek geöffnet?**

c.   **Um wie viel Uhr fährt der Zug nach Freiburg?**

d.   **Wann kommen Sie in München an?**

e.   **Um wie viel Uhr kommen die Nachrichten?**

6. Can you write sentences following the same pattern as the example?

Example: **Rechts abbiegen.**   *Biegen Sie rechts ab.*

a. **In Mannheim umsteigen.**

b. **Geradeaus fahren, dann links einbiegen.**

c. **Das Geld einwerfen.**

d. **Den Fahrschein im Bus entwerten.**

e. **Um elf Uhr abfahren.**

7. There are eight compound nouns in this string of letters. Each word overlaps with its neighbor by one letter. Can you find the nouns?

**RENNFAHRERUHETAGELDAUTOMATAXISTANDAMENMODERDGES
CHOSSCHREIBWARENLADENEUSEELAND**

1.

2.

3.

4.

5.

6.

7.

8.

Answer Key

1. 1. hello, 2. hello, 3. goodbye, 4. hello, 5. goodbye, 6. goodbye; 1. uncertain, 2. morning, 3. uncertain, 4. evening, 5. uncertain, 6. night

2. anytime: Auf Wiedersehen!, Tschüs!; morning: Guten Tag!, Guten Morgen!; evening: Guten Abend!, night: Gute Nacht!

3. Sample Answers: 1. Guten Morgen, Frau Unsinn./Ach, Morgen, Christian.; 2. Guten Tag, Herr Springer./Hallo, Florian.; 3. Guten Abend, Werner./Abend Bernd.; 4. Auf Wiedersehen, Sandra./Gute Nacht Helen.

4. Answers will vary.

5. 1. c + 1; 2. a + 3; 3. b + 2

6. Guten Tag. /heiße (your name)./Familienname (last name)./Vorname, (first name).

7. geht es Ihnen; gut, danke; Ihnen

LESSON 2

1. Steuer, Gross, Schmäh, Schmitt

2. Answers will vary.

3. P-E-T-R-A, K-L-A-U-S, S-A-B-I-N-E, S-Y-L-V-I-A, K-A-Umlaut-T-H-E, W-E-R-N-E-R

4. Answers will vary.

5. Answers will vary.

6. Tempo Magazin, Dieter Schulz; ABC Werbung, Petra Lenz

7. Answers will vary.

8. A–Z 314 8919; Marion 894 7282; Rudi 782 0407; Gudrun Pfaff 815 7482 (correct)

9. a. Guten Tag. Mein Name ist Henneberg – Horst Henneberg.; b. Guten Abend, Herr Schmidt! Wie geht es Ihnen?; c. Guten Morgen. Ich bin Fritz Knoll.; d. Kommen Sie herein.

10. 1. a) ich buchstabiere; b) Sie buchstabieren; c) wir buchstabieren
    2. a) ihr wiederholt; b) sie wiederholt; c) du wiederholst
    3. a) du hörst zu; b) er hört zu; c) ich höre zu
    4. a) sie ruft zurück; b) Sie rufen zurück; c) wir rufen zurück

11. Singular: ich heiße, du heißt, Sie heißen, er heißt, sie heißt, es heißt, Sie heißen
    Plural: wir heißen, ihr heißt, Sie heißen, sie heißen

12. Answers will vary.

1. Herr Schwarz: Wien, Frau Müller: München, Frau Hansen: Kiel, Herr Krüger: Berlin; Vienna, Munich, Kiel, Berlin

2. Herr Schwarz: Wien, Frau Müller: München, Frau Hansen: Kiel, Herr Krüger: Berlin

3. ich komme, du kommst, Sie kommen, er/sie/es kommt, wir kommen, ihr kommt, sie kommen

4. Susan Bell kommt aus den USA, aus New York., Dieter Pohl kommt aus Wien., Herr Nowakowski kommt aus Polen., Otto Hinze kommt aus Bern.

5. Answers will vary.

6. Answers will vary.

7. Answers will vary.

8. 1. Zwei plus vier ist sechs. 2 + 4 = 6; 2. Fünf minus zwei ist drei. 5 – 2 = 3; 3. Sieben plus fünf ist zwölf. 7 + 5 = 12; 4. Achtzehn minus acht ist zehn. 18 – 8 = 10; 5. Zwanzig minus sieben ist dreizehn. 20 – 7 = 13; 6. Siebzehn minus acht ist neun. 17 – 8 = 9

9. Fluggesellschaft: AA, Flugnummer: AA1230, Ziel: New York; Fluggesellschaft: BA, Flugnummer: BA456, Ziel: London Heathrow; Fluggesellschaft: QA, Flugnummer: QA2370, Ziel: Sydney; Fluggesellschaft: LH, Flugnummer: LH7245, Ziel: Moskau; Fluggesellschaft: AF, Flugnummer: AF1170, Ziel: Paris; Fluggesellschaft: LH, Flugnummer: LH7256, Ziel: Rom

10. Answers will vary.

LESSON 4

1. Eine Bratwurst mit Brot und eine Cola.

2. Bitte; möchte; Bratwurst; Sonst; eine Cola; danke

3. Answers will vary.

4. Ich möchte eine Bratwurst mit Brot und eine Currywurst.;
   Ja, eine Portion Pommes frites.;
   Nein, danke.

5. 1. Ich möchte eine Currywurst; 2. Ich möchte ein kleines Bier; 3. Ich möchte ein Käsebrot; 4. Ich möchte eine Cola or Ich möchte ein großes Bier or Ich möchte eine Bratwurst mit Brot

6. Answers will vary.

7. 1. 1,20€; 2. 3,50€; 3. 18€; 4. 80€; 5. 30€; 6. 13,10€; 7. 40,50€; 8. 17€; 9. 7,70€; 10. 9,90€

LESSON 5

1. Table 1: einen Ceylon-Tee mit Zitrone, Table 2: einen Filterkaffee, Table 3: ein großes Pils, Table 4: einen Orangensaft

2. Answers will vary.

3. a. C; b. D; c. B; d. A

4. 1. Zwei Glas Tee und ein Kännchen Kaffee.; 2. Zwei kleine Pils, einen Cappuccino und eine Apfelschorle.; 3. Ein Mineralwasser und einen Espresso.

5. a. (Ich möchte) einen Tee (bitte). b. (Ich möchte) einen Kaffee (bitte). c. (Ich möchte) ein Bier (bitte). d. (Ich möchte) einen Orangensaft (bitte).

6. Ich möchte/Ich hätte gern… 1. einen Apfelsaft, 2. einen Cappuccino, 3. einen Espresso, 4. ein Export, 5. einen Fruchtsaft, 6. ein Kännchen, 7. eine Milch, 8. einen Orangensaft, 9. ein Pils, 10. eine heiße Schokolade.

7. Answers will vary.

8. Answers will vary.

LESSON 6

1. Rosen, Vollkornbrot; sechs Rosen, ein großes Vollkornbrot

2. 1. "Käthes Blumen" 2. "Bäckerei Moritz" 3. "Souvenirs" 4. "Käse"
   5. "Obst & Gemüse"

3. Answers will vary.

4. 1. Guten Tag. Haben Sie Edamer Käse?; Ich nehme vierhundert Gramm.;
   Nein, danke. 2. Guten Tag. Haben Sie schwarze Oliven?; Ich nehme hundert
   Gramm.; Nein, danke. 3. Guten Tag. Haben Sie Orangen?; Ich nehme fünf
   Stück.; Nein, danke. 4. Guten Tag. Haben Sie Nektarinen?; Ich nehme fünf
   Stück.; Nein, danke.

5. fünfundzwanzig, sechsundzwanzig, siebenundzwanzig, achtundzwanzig,
   neunundzwanzig, dreißig, einunddreißig, zweiunddreißig, dreiunddreißig,
   vierunddreißig, fünfunddreißig, sechsunddreißig, siebenunddreißig,
   achtunddreißig, neununddreißig, vierzig

6. a. 34; b. 30; c. 79; d. 35; e. 28; f. 62; g. 93; h. 18; i. 41; j. 65

7. Answers will vary.

8. Answers will vary.

1. verheiratet, ledig, geschieden, einen Partner haben, getrennt

2. 1. one daughter; 2. one son; 3. two sons; 4. no children; 5. one son and two daughters; 6. no children

3. a. Mutter; b. Vater; c. Bruder; d. Mann; e. Schwester; f. Schwester, g. Sohn; h. Tochter

4. habe, hat, haben, haben, haben

5. meine;   my family
   meine;   my mother
   meine;   my grandchildren

   unsere;   our brothers
   unsere;   our brothers and sisters
   unsere;   our grandmother
   unser;   our child

   eure;   your wives
   eure;   your husbands
   eure;   your sister
   euer;   your father

   ihre   their parents
   ihr   their son
   ihre   their daughter
   ihr   their grandfather

6. Answers will vary.

7. a. Nein, ihre Eltern heißen Hedwig und Clemens.; b. Nein, ihre Schwestern heißen Birgit und Steffi.; c. Ihre Tochter heißt Julia.; d. Ja, ihr Mann heißt Klaus.; e. Nein, ihr Sohn heißt Raphael.

LESSON 8

1. in einer Bank, in einer Schule, in einem Geschäft

2. 1. Katharina Müller ist Architektin. (architect), 2. Jochen Weiß ist Fotograf. (photographer), 3. Klaus-Dieter Stolz ist Kundenberater. (customer adviser), 4. Paula Prescher ist Ärztin. (doctor), 5. Stefan Dombrowski ist Computertechniker. (technician)

3. a. Dieter Speck ist Taxifahrer. Er ist kein … (Answers will vary. Example: Künstler) b. Sonja Brückner ist Friseurin. Sie ist keine … c. Rudi Dessau ist Bauarbeiter. Er ist kein … d. Andreas Freitag ist Kassierer. Er ist kein …

4. 1. a; 2. d; 3. f; 4. b; 5. c; 6. e

5. a. Ja, ich bin Kellner/Kellnerin. (restaurant) b. Ja, ich bin Verkäufer/ Verkäuferin. (store) c. Ja, ich bin Lehrer/Lehrerin. (school) d. Ja, ich bin Professor/Professorin. (university) e. Ja, ich bin Kassierer/Kassiererin. (bank) f. Ja, ich bin Arzt/Ärztin or Krankenpfleger/Krankenpflegerin. (hospital) (If you know other job titles, you may have different answers.)

6. Answers will vary.

7. Sample Answers: 1. Ich heiße … 2. Ich komme aus … 3. Ja, ich bin verheiratet./Nein, ich bin nicht verheiratet. 4. Ich bin … 5. Ich arbeite …

LESSON 9

1. Englisch, Französisch, Italienisch, Türkisch, Russisch, Polnisch

2. German (Deutsch); Polish (Polnisch); English (Englisch); Russian (Russisch); French (Französisch);, Spanish (Spanisch); Italian (Italienisch); Turkish (Türkisch)

3. Deutsch: Deutscher/Deutsche, Österreicher/in, Schweizer/in; Englisch: Amerikaner/in, Australier/in, Brite/Britin, Kanadier/in; Französisch: Franzose/Französin, Kanadier/in, Schweizer/in; Italienisch: Italiener/in, Schweizer/in; Polnisch: Pole/Polin; Russisch: Russe/Russin; Spanisch: Spanier/in; Türkisch: Türke/Türkin

4. a. Land: Österreich; Muttersprache: Deutsch; Fremdsprachen: etwas Italienisch; Alter: 25; Familienstand: ledig; b. Staatsangehörigkeit: türkisch; Muttersprache: Türkisch; Fremdsprachen: Englisch; Alter: 27; c. Land: Deutschland; Staatsangehörigkeit: schweizerisch; Fremdsprachen: Englisch, Französisch; Familienstand: geschieden

5. Answers will vary.

6. Answers will vary.

7. 1. Achim und Helen sprechen Polnisch., 2. Herr Bünchen, sprechen Sie Italienisch?, 3. Sandra und ich, wir sprechen Spanisch., 4. Astrid und Bernd sprechen Englisch., 5. Frau Springer, sprechen Sie Deutsch?, 6. Florian spricht Türkisch.

8. Answers will vary.

TEST 1

1. 1. CURRYWURST; 2. STÜCK; 3. KÄNNCHEN; 4. PROBIEREN; 5. BIER; 6. ICH;
   7. WURST; 8. SAHNE; 9. HABEN; 10. SEIN; 11. ETWAS

2. a. siebenunddreißig; b. zweiundsechzig; c. neununddreißig; d. fünfundfünfzig;
   e. dreiundzwanzig

3. a. ist, kommt, spricht, ist, hat, heißt; b. heiße, komme, spreche, bin, habe;
   c. bin, ist, kommen, haben, heißen

4. a. Sylvia kommt aus England. Sie ist Engländerin. Sie spricht Englisch.;
   b. Bob kommt aus den USA. Er ist Amerikaner. Er spricht Englisch.;
   c. Jasmin kommt aus der Türkei. Sie ist Türkin. Sie spricht Türkisch.;
   d. Hans kommt aus Deutschland. Er ist Deutscher. Er spricht Deutsch.;
   e. Isabelle kommt aus Frankreich. Sie ist Französin. Sie spricht Französisch.;
   f. Marco kommt aus Italien. Er ist Italiener. Er spricht Italienisch.;
   g. Will kommt aus Australien. Er ist Australier. Er spricht Englisch.;
   h. Mikhail kommt aus Russland. Er ist Russe. Er spricht Russisch.;
   i. Delphine kommt aus der Schweiz. Sie ist Schweizerin. Sie spricht Französisch.;
   j. Erika kommt aus Österreich. Sie ist Österreicherin. Sie spricht Deutsch.

5. 1. Tochter, Söhne; 2. Geschwister, Schwester, Bruder; 3. Mann; 4. Kinder;
   5. Mutter, Vater; 6. Großmutter, Großvater; 7. Frau; 8. Enkelkinder

6. a. Dieter Hanschke ist Bauarbeiter.; b. Jürgen Schumacher ist Friseur.; c. Birgit
   Harms ist Lehrerin.; d. Uwe Balzer ist Krankenpfleger.; e. Renate Bachmann
   ist Kassiererin.

7.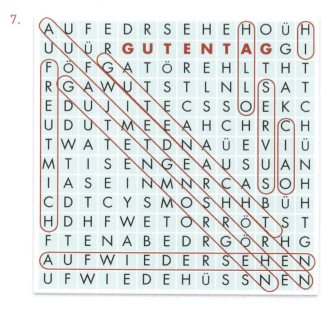

LESSON 10

1. Herr Bachmann: Zimmer 123; Frau Armbruster: Zimmer 117

2. Herr Bader: Zimmer 217; Frau Reisner: Zimmer 219

3. 201 zweihunderteins; 221 zweihunderteinundzwanzig; 199 (ein)hundertneunundneunzig; 257 zweihundertsiebenundfünfzig; 375 dreihundertfünfundsiebzig; 999 neunhundertneunundneunzig

4. 1. 80€, 110€, ja, ja, ja; 2. 60€, 75€, ja, ja, ja; 3. 90€, 120€, not given, not given, nein

5. Ja, haben Sie ein Doppelzimmer frei?; Drei Nächte.; Ist Frühstück inklusive?; Ich nehme es. (Wir nehmen es.)

6. Sample Answers: Familienname: Kowalski, Vorname: Robert, Anschrift Straße/Nummer: 1234 Bright Street, PLZ/Wohnort: 10098 New York, Land: USA, Ausweisnummer: 019670084

7. Sample Answers: 1. Was kostet ein Doppelzimmer pro Nacht?, Und was kostet ein Einzelzimmer?, Ist Frühstück inklusive?, Und ist das Zimmer mit Bad?, Gut. Danke. Wiedersehen.; 2. Haben Sie zwei Einzelzimmer frei? Das ist sehr teuer!, Haben Sie ein Doppelzimmer frei?, Oje! Das ist auch sehr teuer. Ist Frühstück wenigstens inklusive?

8. 1. Zimmer vierhundertvierundsiebzig. 2. Ich habe ein Zimmer reserviert. 3. Ich reise heute ab. 4. Ich möchte ein Doppelzimmer mit Dusche. 5. Haben Sie Zimmer frei?

LESSON 11

1. eine Post, ein Restaurant, ein Café

2. a. 1. die Post, 2. der Zeitungshändler; b. 6. der Blumenladen; c. 4. das Restaurant; d. 3. das Café, 4. das Restaurant; e. 2. der Zeitungshändler, 7. die Buchhandlung; f. 1. die Post, 5. die Bank, 8. der Geldautomat

3. a. eine; b. ein; c. ein; d. eine; e. ein; f. ein; g. eine; h. ein

4. 1. a; 2. c; 3. b; 4. d; 5. d; 6. e; 7. a; 8. c

5. 1. c (Hotel Spreewald) 2. b (Café Dreiklang) 3. a (U-Bahn-Station Uhlandstraße) 4. e (Bäckerei) 5. d (Taxistand) 6. f (Telefonzelle)

6. a. Wie bitte? b. Wie war das noch mal? c. Langsamer, bitte! d. Wie heißt die Straße? e. Können Sie das buchstabieren? f. Ich verstehe nicht.

7. a. Gedächtniskirche; b. Siegessäule; c. Kongresshalle; d. Brandenburger Tor. The Fernsehturm (television tower) is the one which doesn't belong: it's on Alexanderplatz, further to the east.

8. Sample Answer:
Hallo,
direkt in meiner Straße gibt es ein gutes Restaurant. Wenn Du aus meinem Haus gehst und die Straße geradeaus weiter läufst, siehst Du nach 600 m auf der linken Seite das Restaurant *Zur Linde*. Von hier ist es nicht weit zum nächsten Geldautomaten und zur Post: Du musst nur hinter dem Restaurant *Zur Linde* links abbiegen und dann an der zweiten Kreuzung rechts. Dort siehst Du auf der linken Straßenseite den Geldautomaten, und gegenüber ist die nächste Post.
Viele Grüße und bis bald
Clara

9. 1. (die) Blumen/(der) Laden, 2. (das) Buch/(die) Handlung, 3. (das) Geld/(der) Automat, 4. (das) Taxi/(der) Stand, 5. (die) U-Bahn/(die) Station, 6. (die) Zeitung/(s)/(der) Händler

1. 6:30 a.m., 8:00 a.m.

2. a. ein, b. zwei., c. fünf, d. neun, e. ein, f. zwei, g. drei, h. vier

3. 1. 13.30; 2. 15.00; 3. 19.30; 4. 22.00

4. a. Montag; b. Dienstag; c. Mittwoch; d. Donnerstag; e. Freitag; f. Samstag/ Sonnabend; g. Sonntag

5. 1. Universitäts-Bibliothek; 2. Stadtmuseum; 3. Touristen-Information

6. Sample Answer: Wir haben montags geschlossen. dienstags bis donnerstags haben wir von zwölf bis fünfzehn Uhr und von siebzehn bis zweiundzwanzig Uhr geöffnet. Freitags und samstags haben wir von zwölf bis fünfzehn Uhr und von siebzehn bis vierundzwanzig Uhr geöffnet. Und sonntags nur von zwölf bis fünfzehn Uhr.

7. Wir haben montags bis freitags von neun (Uhr) bis sechzehn Uhr geöffnet. Wir haben samstags/sonnabends von neun (Uhr) bis achtzehn Uhr geöffnet. Sonntags haben wir geschlossen. (It would also be correct to say: "Sonntag ist Ruhetag.")

8. a. E; b. C; c. D; d. B; e. A

1. 1. ein Kugelschreiber (a ballpoint pen), 2. eine Zeitung (a newspaper), 3. Kopfschmerztabletten (aspirin)

2. a. Wo kann ich (hier) eine Zeitung kaufen? b. Wo kann ich (hier) einen Kugelschreiber kaufen? c. Wo kann ich (hier) Kopfschmerztabletten kaufen? d. Wo kann ich (hier) Obst kaufen? e. Wo kann ich (hier) Briefmarken kaufen? f. Wo kann ich (hier) Brot kaufen?

3. a. Obsthändler; b. Bäckerei; c. Zeitungshändler; d. Apotheke; e. Schreibwarenladen; f. Post

4. 1. none, 2. die zweite Straße links und die erste Straße rechts, 3. none, 4. die erste links., 5. none, 6. die zweite Straße links, dann die zweite rechts.

5. a. Gehen Sie die zweite Straße rechts und dann die erste Straße links. Dort ist ein Café. b. Gehen Sie die dritte Straße links. Dort ist ein Supermarkt. c. Gehen Sie die zweite Straße links und dann die zweite rechts. Die Bäckerei ist an der Ecke. (You may have phrased your answers slightly differently.)

6. ETAGENPLAN: Erdgeschoss: Kosmetika und Parfümerie (US: first floor)
erste Etage: Damenmode und Damenwäsche (US: second floor)
zweite Etage: Herrenmode und Herrenwäsche (US: third floor)
dritte Etage: Haushaltswaren und Porzellan (US: fourth floor)
vierte Etage: Spielwaren und Sportartikel (US: fifth floor)
fünfte Etage: Elektrogeräte und Computer (US: sixth floor)
sechste Etage: Dachterrassencafé (US: seventh floor)

7. Answers will vary.

8. Answers will vary.

1. ein Hemd; es ist viel zu modern.

2. rotate the wheel two times (clockwise)

3. 1. hair: kurz und dunkel 2. jacket: weiß und rot 3. sweater: orange
   4. skirt: blau 5. shoes: rot

4. Bluse, Stil, Farbe, weiße, Größe

5. 1. große, gestreiftes, gemustertes, einfaches, weißes, schönes, modern.
   2. bestimmten, bestimmte, schlichte, weiße, gute, schlank

6. 1. a. -en (weißen); b. -e (weiße); c. -es (weißes); 2. a. -en (schlichten); b. -e
   (schlichte); c. -es (schlichtes); 3. a. die grüne, b. rote, c. schönes

7. Sample answer: blaues; rote; orange; grünen; rosarote; gelben; weiße; grüne

8. a. Ich suche eine blaue Hose. Ich habe Größe [your size]. b. Ich suche ein
   grünes Hemd. Ich habe Größe [your size].

LESSON 15

1. für ihre kleine Nichte, für ihren Mann

2. a. Im dritten Stock; b. In der vierten Etage; c. Im Erdgeschoss

3. a. Im fünften Stock./In der fünften Etage./Im fünften Geschoss.;
   b. Im zweiten Stock./In der zweiten Etage./Im zweiten Geschoss.;
   c. Im Erdgeschoss.; d. Im ersten Stock./In der ersten Etage./Im ersten Geschoss.

4. Er nimmt den kleinen Teddy, die mittelgroße Puppe, das rosarote Schweinchen und die kleinen Autos.

5. Positive: Ausgezeichnet! Klasse! Prima! Toll! Wunderschön!; Negative: Hässlich! Igitt! Schrecklich!

6. Answers will vary.

7. Doesn't want: eine schöne Party oder große Torte; wants: ein Handy oder eine Digitalkamera oder eine Reise (nach Hawaii oder Südafrika)

8. Anke wants a bookcase filled with books. Rabea wants lots of chocolate or a new car.

9. Answers will vary.

LESSON 16

1. Düsseldorf, Magdeburg

2. 1. 11:07 to Düsseldorf, 2. 11:40 to Magdeburg, 3. 12:09 to Düsseldorf, 4. 11:56 to Köln

3. Hallo, Ich fahre mit dem Eurocity Nummer 32 nach Berlin, planmäßige Abfahrt 12:10 Uhr von Gleis sieben.

4. 1. h; 2. c; 3. f; 4. a; 5. d; 6. c

5. a. Der Zug fährt um 11:46 (elf Uhr sechsundvierzig). b. Man muss in Mannheim umsteigen. c. Die Fahrt kostet 137 (einhundertsiebenunddreißig) Euro insgesamt. d. Der Zuschlag kostet 20 (zwanzig) Euro. e. Der Zug fährt auf Gleis zwei ab.

6. Einmal Hamburg-Altona einfach, bitte., Zweite Klasse., (Ich fahre) mit dem ICE.

7. a. Zweimal Berlin, hin und zurück., Zweite Klasse., (Ich fahre) mit dem ICE., Wann fährt der Zug?, Danke. (Auf) Wiedersehen! b. Einmal Frankfurt, einfach, bitte., Erste Klasse., (Ich fahre) mit dem ICE., Wann fährt der Zug?, Danke. (Auf) Wiedersehen!

1. einen Kleinwagen, für drei Tage ab heute.

2. 1. (Klasse B: 80,– € pro Tag x 3 Tage) 240,– €; 2. (Klasse E: 97,– € pro Tag x 14 Tage) 1358,– €

3. Ich möchte einen mittleren Kombi mieten., Für sieben Tage., Bitte schön. Ist das Kilometergeld inbegriffen (inklusive)?

4. 1. Prohibition (dürfen Sie nicht); 2. Prohibition (darf man nicht); 3. Obligation (müssen); 4. Permission (darf ich, Sie dürfen) and obligation (Sie müssen)

5. 1. darf; 2. muss; 3. darf; 4. darf

6. a, b, d

7. Bregenzer Str.

1. Museumsinsel, relatively close

2. a. 7; b. 8; c. 7

3. a. Fahren Sie mit der U2 Richtung Spandau., b. Fahren Sie mit der U2 Richtung Spandau., c. Nehmen Sie die U2 Richtung Spandau bis Potsdamer Platz. Dann nehmen Sie die S1 Richtung Oranienburg.

4. 1. C; 2. B; 3. C; 4. D; 5. D; 6. A

5. Answers will vary.

6. a. Fahrschein im Bus entwerten., b. Geld einwerfen., c. Wechselgeld und Fahrschein entnehmen., d. Fahrschein wählen.

7. Answers will vary.

8. a. Ich kaufe das rote Auto.
   b. Im ersten Stock ist die Drogerie.
   c. Ich möchte eine grüne Bluse und weiße Socken.
   d. Paula nimmt die halbe Portion Pommes und ein ganzes Brot.
   e. Die kleine Puppe trägt ein gelbes Kleid und der große Teddy ein braunes.
   f. Clara und Paul haben beide blaue Augen.
   g. Ich habe einen ähnlichen Pullover.
   h. Herr Marten trägt das schwarze Jackett.

TEST 2

1. Across:
   1. UMSTEIGEN; 3. FAHRSCHEIN; 4. ZURÜCK; 5. VERSICHERUNG;
   6. RICHTUNG; 7. ABFAHRT; 9. GLEIS; 10. EINMAL
   Down:
   2. EINBAHNSTRASSE; 3. FAHRE; 4. ZUSCHLAG; 7. ALLE; 8. GEHEN

2. a. Ich suche einen roten Rock., b. Ich suche eine grüne Hose., c. Ich suche
   eine schwarze Jacke., d. Ich suche ein weißes Hemd., e. Ich suche einen
   blauen Pullover.

3. Elektrogeräte: Computer; Spielwaren: Puppe, Teddy; Schreibwaren:
   Kugelschreiber; Damenmode: Rock, Bluse; Herrenmode: Herrenhose, Schlips;
   Kosmetika: Parfüm; Lebensmittel: Brot, Fleisch

4. Guten Tag. Kann ich etwas für Sie tun?, Ja. Wir möchten ein Doppelzimmer
   mit Dusche., Wie lange möchten Sie bleiben?, Wir möchten drei Nächte
   bleiben., Ja, wir haben ein Doppelzimmer frei. Das kostet einhundertzehn
   Euro pro Nacht., Ist Frühstück inbegriffen?, Ja, Frühstück ist inbegriffen., Wir
   nehmen es., Füllen Sie bitte das Formular aus. OR: Füllen Sie das Formular
   aus, bitte.

5. a. Es ist Viertel nach acht., b. Die Bibliothek ist von neun Uhr dreißig bis
   neunzehn Uhr dreißig geöffnet., c. Der Zug nach Freiburg fährt um siebzehn
   Uhr zehn., d. Ich komme (Wir kommen) um halb sechs in München an.,
   e. Die Nachrichten kommen um Viertel vor sechs.

6. a. Steigen Sie in Mannheim um., b. Fahren Sie geradeaus, biegen Sie dann
   links ein., c. Werfen Sie das Geld ein., d. Entwerten Sie den Fahrschein im
   Bus., e. Fahren Sie um elf Uhr ab.

7. Rennfahrer, Ruhetag, Geldautomat, Taxistand, Damenmode, Erdgeschoss,
   Schreibwarenladen, Neuseeland

Photo Credits

LESSON 1

(7) Zsolt Nyulaszi.Shutterstock.2008

(9) Kurhan.Shutterstock.2010

(11) Andresr.Shutterstock.2010, Yuri Arcurs.Shutterstock.2010, oliveromg. Shutterstock.2010, Kovalchynskyy Mykola.Shutterstock.2010

(12) Yuri Arcurs.Shutterstock.2010

(13) Yuri Arcurs.Shutterstock.2010, iofoto.Shutterstock.2010, Olga Sapegina.Shutterstock.2010

LESSON 2

(17) Orange Line Media.Shutterstock.2010

(18) Andresr.Shutterstock.2010, StockLite.Shutterstock.2010, T-Design. Shutterstock.2010, Yuri Arcurs.Shutterstock.2010, Rui Vale de Sousa.Shutterstock.2010, Jason Stitt.Shutterstock.2010

(27) Karen Roach.Shutterstock.2010

LESSON 3

(29) StockLite.Shutterstock.2010

(32) Andresr.Shutterstock.2010, doglikehorse.Shutterstock.2010, T-Design.Shutterstock.2010, Ivan Jelisavic.Shutterstock.2010

LESSON 4

(39) Createsta.Shutterstock.2010

(40) Valua Vitaly.Shutterstock.2010, Kurhan.Shutterstock.2010

LESSON 5

(47) Vasiliy Koval.Shutterstock.2010

(50) Terence Mendoza.Shutterstock.2010, Phil Date.Shutterstock.2010, Leah-Anne Thompson.Shutterstock.2010, ©iStockphoto.com/Sean Locke. Shutterstock.2010

LESSON 6

(55) ©2010 Fotolia/Alan Reed

(59) Kurhan.Shutterstock.2010

(62) ©iStockphoto.com/Jiri Moucka

LESSON 7

(65) Monkey Business Images.Shutterstock.2010

(67) Julie Keen.Shutterstock.2010

(69) Carme Balcells.Shutterstock.2010, Yuri Arcurs.Shutterstock.2010, Kurhan. Shutterstock.2010, Lisa F. Young.Shutterstock.2010, Rocketclips, Inc. Shutterstock.2010, Jacek Chabraszewski.Shutterstock.2010

Photo Credits

LESSON 8

(75) J C Fedele.Shutterstock.2010

(79) Konstantin Sutyagin.Shutterstock.2010, dean bertoncelj.Shutterstock.2010, Igor S. Srdanovic.Shutterstock.2010, mangostock.Shutterstock.2010

(80) Stephen Mahar.Shutterstock.2010, Pefkos.Shutterstock.2010, Noah Strycker. Shutterstock.2010, ©iStockphoto.com/Mlenny Photography/ Alexander Hafemann, Cynthia Farmer.Shutterstock.2010, ©iStockphoto.com/fotoVoyager

LESSON 9

(83) Andresr.Shutterstock.2010

(84) Andresr.Shutterstock.2010, Shippee.Shutterstock.2010, Rui Vale de Sousa. Shutterstock.2010, Kurhan.Shutterstock.2010, Andriianov.Shutterstock.2010

(91) Jacek Chabraszewski.Shutterstock.2010, Andresr.Shutterstock.2010, Iakov Filimonov.Shutterstock.2010, ostill.Shutterstock.2010, NicolasMcComber. Shutterstock.2010

LESSON 10

(99) fotorobs.Shutterstock.2010

(103) ©iStockphoto.com/AndreasWeber

(104) Sandra Gligorijevic.Shutterstock.2010

LESSON 11

(109) DieAugenweide.Shutterstock.2010

(117) Yuri Arcurs.Shutterstock.2010

LESSON 12

(121) Philip Lange.Shutterstock.2010

(122) ©iStockphoto.com/Rtimages, ©iStockphoto.com/joshblake

(124) Yuri Arcurs.Shutterstock.2010

LESSON 13

(131) ©iStockphoto.com/webphotographer

(134) i9370.Shutterstock.2010, Antonov Roman.Shutterstock.2010, tuulijumala.Shutterstock.2010, ostromec.Shutterstock.2010, VGB.Shutterstock.2010, Jason Swalwell.Shutterstock.2010

LESSON 14

(141) Gladskikh Tatiana.Shutterstock.2010

(142) Kurhan.Shutterstock.2010

(148) UrosK.Shutterstock.2010, Elliot Westacott.Shutterstock.2010

(149) Andriianov.Shutterstock.2010

LESSON 15

[151] Diego Cervo.Shutterstock.2010

[152] Kurhan.Shutterstock.2010, Franco's photos.Shutterstock.2010

[155] J. Helgason.Shutterstock.2010, Arsgera.Shutterstock.2010, Edd
Westmacott.Shutterstock.2010, Barnaby Chambers.Shutterstock.2010, Yuri
Arcurs.Shutterstock.2010

[158] Yuri Arcurs.Shutterstock.2010, Andresr.Shutterstock.2010

LESSON 16

[161] ©iStockphoto.com/melhi

[163] Regien Paassen.Shutterstock.2010

LESSON 17

[171] ©2010 Fotolia/lite

[173] ©iStockphoto.com/1001nights

[175] Maksim Toome.Shutterstock.2010

LESSON 18

[183] Philip Lange.Shutterstock.2010

[184] mathom.Shutterstock.2010, Elena Elisseeva.Shutterstock.2010

[188] Andresr.Shutterstock.2010, Yuri Arcurs.Shutterstock.2010, Rul Vale de
Sousa.Shutterstock.2010

Make **Berlitz**® the first word of your second language.

Berlitz® expands your world with travel and language-learning products in hundreds of destinations and more than 30 languages.

The Language Experts

Available at your local bookseller or
www.berlitzpublishing.com